THE GARDEN DESIGN BOOK

THE GARDEN

DESIGN BOOK

by
cheryl merser
and the
editors of
garden design
magazine

THE GARDEN DESIGN BOOK.
Copyright © 1997
by Meigher Communications, L.P.
All rights reserved.
Printed in the United States of America
No part of this book may be used
or reproduced in any manner whatsoever
without written permission except
in the case of brief quotations embodied
in critical articles and reviews.
For information address HarperCollins
Publishers, Inc., 10 East 53rd Street,
New York, NY 10022.

HarperCollins books may be purchased
for educational, business, or sales
promotional use. For information please
write: Special Markets Department,
HarperCollins Publishers, Inc.,
10 East 53rd Street, New York, NY 10022.

FIRST EDITION

Designed by Helene Silverman

ISBN 0-06-039207-X

98 99 00 01 / WZ 10 9 8 7 6 5 4 3 2

contents

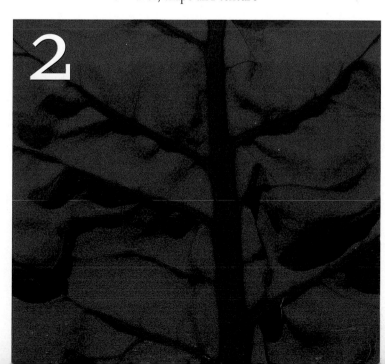

1

THE NEW GARDENER

2

THE FIVE SENSES

3

THE ESSENTIAL DESIGN ELEMENTS

FOREWORD

If you're the kind of person who drools over drop-dead-gorgeous photographs in most garden books, but are stumped when you try to apply their glossy dreams to the plot of ground at your feet, welcome to a different kind of book. Sure, it's packed with glorious images, but this book does not stop there. It takes those dreams and spins them out, in real-time and real-life. When Meigher Communications bought GARDEN DESIGN magazine and relaunched it in 1994, we were convinced that millions of new gardeners—a whole generation of them—were discovering the garden, people with more style than time, more enthusiasm than expertise. Beyond the magazine, we believed these new gardeners needed a definitive resource of ideas and inspiration, packaged just for them. THE GARDEN DESIGN BOOK helps readers look at their gardens in a new way, and helps them confront certain awesome truths: Plants are much more than their flowers, and gardens are much more than their plants.

In Cheryl Merser we found a perceptive, real human being—a gardener and a writer—whose voice brims with warmth and the excitement of discovery. This book belongs to Douglas Brenner, too, Editor of the magazine. Doug's impassioned intelligence and elegant style shaped the book's spirit (and letter). Creative Director Michael Grossman once again got the glory onto the page, working with the fine eye of the book's designer, Helene Silverman. Others on our core team: Art Director Christin Gangi, Photo Editor Lauren Hicks, major liaison Cristina Roig Morris, and majordomo Catherine Vail. The book draws on the best work of the magazine's photographers, editors, horticulturists, illustrators, and gardeners—especially Christopher Hirsheimer, Denise Otis, Dora Galitzki, Jack Ruttle, Sarah Gray Miller, Stephanie Woodard, Holly Lynton, Melissa Moss, Betsey Barnum, Harriet Heyman, Susan Heeger, Stephen Scanniello—and a crack research, copy, and design team: Amy Calabrese, John Haney, Doan Hoang, Carly Hutchinson, Nanette Maxim, Ann McCarthy, George Stone, Neal Boulton, and Stacie Reistetter. Thanks to them and to all Meigher Communications employee-partners who make our company culture the best; and to President Doug Peabody, Publishing Director extraordinaire Joe Armstrong, and especially to our Chairman, Chris Meigher (Cid, here's your first spoke). At HarperCollins and Regan Books, we had the unbounded enthusiasm of Judith Regan, the exquisite stewardship of Kristin Kiser, and the great luck of Larry Ashmead's generosity. —*Dorothy Kalins,* Editor-in-Chief, GARDEN DESIGN

PLANTS AS DESIGN TOOLS

PLANS FOR THE WHOLE GARDEN

THE NEW GARDENER

I

who is the new gardener?

what is the new garden?

how does the garden grow?

WHEN I first took up gardening, I rarely talked about it with my friends, no more than I would have made it known that I'd taken up, say, bingo, shuffleboard, bullfighting, or any other dubious, out-of-the-mainstream weekend pursuit. In my world back then, a world of urban young people dressed for success

Who is the new gardener?

and scrambling to claim a sturdy foothold on a crowded ladder, even the pace of gardening—which is to say, the pace that the seasons set—would have seemed absurdly slow, irrelevant, and incongruous with the business at hand, that of inventing our grown-up lives. We all moved too fast to stop and garden. If anything, I suppose I might have felt that being drawn to the garden would have been admitting to a weakness, stating somehow that I wasn't up to the fast track after all.

Besides, who gardened back then—fifteen, eighteen, twenty years ago? Only stereotypes, as far as I knew: English people, certainly, no-nonsense women in tweeds, energetically calling their neat cottage gardens to attention, the way they might have done in a Barbara Pym novel. Older people closer to home—women attending to ivy and geraniums in window boxes, or retired men puttering among the tomatoes. Eccentrics, muttering to their plants to perk them up, and the few remaining quirky souls in this world who still spoke Latin to one another. Rich people had gardens, but that was because they had gardeners. Sub-urbanites, the ones I grew up among any-way, didn't garden, exactly, although they did mow their lawns (or have the

The doyenne of British garden design, Gertrude Jekyll (1843–1932) had a staff of four to tend her five acres of impeccable perennial borders and cultivated woodland. Though still widely admired on this side of the Atlantic, Jekyll set exacting standards for color harmony and continuous bloom that few modern homeowners have the time or the inclination to attain.

13

The new gardeners include, *(from left):* Undaunted conquerors of limited space like Kerry Trueman and Matthew Rosenberg, on their Manhattan rooftop; self-taught experimentalists like topiary master Pearl Fryar, in his South Carolina yard; passionate amateur farmers like artist Gary Craig, of Yelm, Washington (see page 258); inventive professionals like architect Dale Booher and garden designer Lisa Stamm (see their collaborative efforts on pages 90 and 139); hands-on horticulturists like rosarian Stephen Scanniello; and pioneers in outdoor living like landscape designer Diane Sjoholm, with her daughter, Daria.

neighbor's teenager do it). They mostly complained about the inevitable crabgrass, and clipped wayward hedges here and there. They may also have tinkered with a few hybrid tea roses or perennials, planted some spring bulbs, and set out pots of splashy annuals come summer; petunias were big, I remember, but the now ubiquitous impatiens were unknown back then.

There are plenty of gardeners today, I'm sure, who grew up with gardening in their blood, who knew from a young age that they would one day have a rose garden like

their grandfather's, a perennial border like their
mother's, or a dark green, cool, wooded place,
with ferns marking the edge of a path through a grove,
that would re-create some magical childhood memory. I
sometimes envied these people, with horticultural visions
already in their blood. On the other hand, there's something to be said for stumbling upon gardening unawares in
the way I did, in the way most gardeners seem to do,
when the wonder and beauty—and the possibilities—hit
you all at once. For me, the sequence was simple: I met a

Elements of garden style enrich our domestic surroundings in unexpected ways. The pattern of an Iranian "garden rug," above, woven in Kurdistan around 1800, is based on the geometric layout of paths, plantings, pools, and outer walls that has shaped Islamic gardens since the seventh century A.D.—and also influenced formal landscape design in medieval Europe. We owe the word "paradise" to *pairidaēza,* ancient Persian for "enclosure" or "park."

man with a house, the house had a garden, and, to my surprise, I found myself spending many happy hours there, at peace and, at the same time, exhilarated in a way I'd never known before. After a few encouraging successes—and many more disasters—I began to figure out what gardening was all about. The more I learned, the more I wanted to know. The more I learned, the more I discovered how much there was to know.

By the time I had a plot of land of my own to cultivate some years later, gardening was no longer my private realm (as if it ever really had been). Who was gardening now? Everyone I knew, or so it seemed. Gardening was suddenly in the air, like a high pollen count during hay fever season. I was amazed. For that matter, Gertrude Jekyll would have been amazed.

From my first go-round, I remembered sleepy garden centers with standard fare: classic perennials, dutiful annuals, roses, assortments of shrubs. Because I had been new to gardening, however, these simple plants had also been new to me, and I learned to love them (or, when I failed them or they failed me, to resent them) one by one, not quite realizing that the plants then available to me didn't begin to cover the full spectrum that nature had to offer.

Americans have a long history of adapting garden ideas gleaned from their travels or from other travelers' souvenirs. A late nineteenth-century stereograph, below, shows Italian-inspired topiary on the Wellesley, Massachusetts, estate of Boston financier Horatio Hollis Hunnewell. Frequently open to the public in Hunnewell's day, the grounds attracted crowds of tourists eager to pick up Italian style secondhand.

And never mind the plants. My reading had taken me to gardens far and wide, ancient gardens, mostly, and over and over again to the majestic herbaceous borders that thrive in England's cool, damp summers. Yet, whatever I read about gardening in those days rarely reminded me of home or showed me what I myself could do. Instead, they were books to dream with, to look at, then to put back on the shelf before I went outside and tried to figure out what to do next.

All of this—from how a garden is conceived to what it can be and what it can do, to what to put into it—was changing. In just a decade, give or take, a new generation of gardeners was beginning to transform this staid old business into a booming new industry, full of energy and new flourishes on classic design. Once you got on one mailing list, catalogs started to arrive almost daily, offering plants, ornaments, furniture, useful (and amazingly useless)

How-to books and magazines on landscape design flooded the market when gardening became a middle-class craze in Victorian Britain and America. Shirley Hibberd's guide *(below)*, published in London in 1856 and soon exported, showed affluent landowners how to follow the latest fashions in flower beds, rockeries, and rose arbors. Today, garden enthusiasts and historians collect such books as works of art and as precious resources for authentic landscape restoration.

paraphernalia for the garden, new books about new ways to garden—you name it. Like casebook studies in supply-and-demand theory, nurseries catered to these new gardeners by offering ever more sophisticated and exotic annuals and perennials, more varieties of shrubs, and then ornamental grasses, which presented a whole new set of possibilities for enhancing even the most formal gardens. Old-fashioned roses—oft spoken of, more nuance than hype—reappeared, as did exquisite tree peonies, about which I had

Maxfield Parrish painted the Villa d'Este (*above*) for Edith Wharton's *Italian Villas and Their Gardens*. The 1904 edition still makes a persuasive case for the architectural clarity, exquisitely simple planting schemes, and timeless romance of classical landscape design.

only read. I began to notice meadows with wildflowers that appeared to be strewn, not planted in rows or drifts. Spring weekends at the garden center began to feel like Filene's Basement at the start of a half-price day. Consumer trend? Maybe, at least in part. But for all the money you can spend on it, gardening isn't something you buy. It's something you do. How you do it depends on who you are, the way you want to live, and the inner vision you wish to express in your garden. How do you develop and refine a personal vision, then successfully transfer it to the soil? That's what this book is about.

If gardening was once a serene, leisure-class activity for people with all the time in the world to garden, it isn't anymore. Among the gardeners I know (and marketing studies back this up), today's most avid gardeners actually have very little leisure time on their hands. Busy professionals, working parents, people who screech into a weekend after living all week at full tilt, find unexpected solace and incomparable pleasure in working the soil— before work, after work, whenever they can find a minute to give to the garden. And

Gardeners often compose plants along the lines of art they admire, be it an Impressionist watercolor or a Chinese scroll, such as this Yuan or Ming Dynasty image of bamboo, below.

a minute to take for themselves, for gardening is a solitary activity, a chance to connect with oneself as much as with the soil, the only time some of us have to play our private tapes or stop to think about absolutely nothing.

Scrapbooks and journals supply fertile ground for the gardener eager to play with new plant combinations or doodle with a tempting trellis or gazebo before it turns into an expensive 3-D mistake. Both veteran and novice gardeners find it helpful to record each season's horticultural successes and failures, for future reference. Individual needs and taste should dictate style and format— an envelope stuffed with empty seed packets, scribbled notes, and catalog clippings may suffice. Elegantly illustrated fill-in-the-blank garden diaries tend to sit on the desk unused. Who wants to soil their pristine pages?

A NUMBER of the most ambitious and inspired gardens I've ever seen (large or small, on a city terrace, a tiny village plot, or rolled out over many country acres) are successful more because of the thinking, planning, and passion that have gone into them than because of the actual hours logged in, season after season. You don't need time, I discovered. You need vision, and vision is something you can learn.

Why have so many of us now taken up gardening? Market analysts commenting on this (literal) growth industry will cite the baby boomers' newfound devotion to hearth and home (to say nothing of home improvement). Is your house too small? One way to enlarge it is by adding garden rooms to expand your living space outdoors. Is your house not appreciating in value the way you hoped or expected it would? A great garden will give it added value, or so one theory goes. Are the Joneses on one side, and the Smiths on the other, creating lovely gardens and making your pathetic minimalist yard look paltry by comparison? Maybe it's time to invest a little in order to keep up.

Market analysts may have part of the story right, but

No matter how many years a gardener has been working the land, he or she feels like a hopeful neophyte all over again when there's a shrub or tree waiting to be put into freshly dug ground. *Opposite:* an oakleaf hydrangea, *H. quercifolia,* stands ready for transplanting. Burlap protects roots surrounded by a ball of the nursery soil in which the shrub started out.

What is the new garden?

Though the concept of the outdoor room has been around for centuries, there are ample opportunities for new variations on the theme. *Above:* A whimsical "carpet," painted on the concrete floor, mixes with eye-catching planters and furniture to transform a bleak New York City rooftop into a stylishly livable terrace.

analysts, with their figures and charts, can't explain why people, once drawn to gardening, find themselves getting in deeper and deeper, reading about gardens they'll never visit, learning about plants they'll never grow, imagining grand or whimsical gardens they may or may not get around to planting. Maybe it's simply because enticing outdoor spaces are cropping up everywhere and, once we see one, we want one of our own; with so many more of us gardening, the garden is that much more accessible and available. Or perhaps the garden is the inevitable antidote to sitting all week in front of a computer screen, or in a noisy, fluorescent-lit office.

Maybe outdoor space is all the more precious because we now have so much less of it.

Or maybe the garden is better celebrated than analyzed. In a consumer society such as ours, gardening is a way to express taste and style while, at the same time, avoiding conspicuous consumption or ostentation—there is a purity to the pursuit. You cannot express yourself by buying a garden. You have to make one.

A wonderful thing about gardening is that, once a garden is in your blood, it's easy to summon it up in your imagination anytime, anyplace. You can escape to your garden during

Contemporary ecological concerns, and appreciation of regional diversity, favor landscaping attuned to native terrain. In Monty and Jocelyn Montgomery's Los Angeles garden *(below)*, a trail lined with rugged vegetation leads the eye into the wilder canyon beyond.

Old rules (flowers in flower beds; edible crops in the vegetable patch) are being tossed aside in gardens like Dean Riddle's exuberant plot, in Phoenicia, New York, where beets and eggplants share beds with angel's trumpet and cosmos.

a boring meeting at work, on the StairMaster, in a traffic jam, waiting in line to get into a movie, in the middle of a snowstorm. You can study catalogs and read books about gardening and plan what you want to do next spring, or the spring after, if you don't get around to it this time.

Once the garden is in place, you can dream about how you want to change it; the further along the garden is, the more elaborate the dreams. Everything about your life can find its way into the garden—colors from a painting you admire; influences from the places you've traveled; the herbs that you enjoy cooking with; a tree to commemorate the birth of a child or the death of a loved one; another sapling that you transplanted when your childhood home was sold, so you'd take a bit of your history with you into tomorrow.

What are the lessons to be learned from a garden or, more to the point, what are the lessons to be learned from this garden book? How to think a garden, both aesthetically and practically, before you plant one. How to make your garden an outgrowth of your house and the way of life it embodies. How to understand garden design as a process, not a onetime blueprint. How to choose among (or mix and match) classic and innovative approaches to design and planting. How to look with new eyes at the garden you've already created, and how to make sure you are expressing the vision you want with the choices you make.

PUT AN AMBITIOUS, instant-gratification-seeking neophyte up against a garden for the first time and there's bound to be trouble. Take my husband, Michael, for example. He's not a gardener (not yet). I spent an entire weekend once, in the first garden we had together, creating a small bed off in a corner in which I wanted to plant a collection of shrubs by a narrow side yard, an alleyway just six feet wide. My idea was to suggest that a path led back there to some interesting scenery; in fact, it led only to the garbage cans.

Like many gardeners, I'd often made the mistake of planting shrubs too close together—they look fine the first year, but by the second or third year, when they begin really filling out, they resemble a horticultural subway car at rush hour: crowded, with no room to stretch out. This time, I didn't make that mistake; I planted the shrubs far enough apart to give them a chance to grow toward one another properly, over time. I had edged the bed diligently and mulched it well; you could see the mulch between the newly planted shrubs. When I finished, I brought Michael out to see what I'd done. "But it doesn't look finished, like

Like the baker who can feel when kneaded dough has just the right consistency, or the tailor who knows whether a worsted has the "hand" to drape just so, the gardener learns to rely on the touch of the soil. Even the supplest goatskin gloves *(opposite)* must at times be taken off for delicate weeding and planting.

How does the garden grow?

a garden," he said, clearly disappointed. "It looks like a shrub sale." I saw a bed that was started, and I knew enough to be able to fill in, with my imagination, what time would do. As I saw it, I had done all I could do; my garden bed was ready for me to turn it over to time. All Michael saw, on the other hand, was a garden that wasn't remotely finished, filled in, luxuriant, or billowing.

Gardeners set their internal clocks by local weather, intuition, and seasonal milestones, like the first snowdrops of spring (below).

To construct a garden, you must first deconstruct everything about the space: the house that the garden will wrap itself around and connect itself to; the land (what's there, what isn't); the vista beyond (whether to draw it into the garden, or to obscure it); what the gardener, given his or her available time and resources, wants the garden to be and to do. There are priorities to set: what to do now, what to get to later. Then, once you've built and planted, there are nuances to consider—everything from where to hang that little birdhouse someone gave you to what kind of ground cover should edge that woodland azalea-lined path to how it will actually feel to be in the garden, to live there, to dine there, to entertain there, to celebrate occasions there: how to make the garden home.

Gardening is a rare process in that there's a beginning and a middle, but no end: a garden is never finished. This is a hard lesson to learn; at least it is for those of us who wouldn't serve a meal only partly cooked, for example, or wear clothing that hasn't been hemmed, or do any home repair work halfway. Gardening is the ultimate nature-versus-nurture equation: How much can the human being do? A lot, but only a part of it even so. One is reminded of the old television commercial for margarine, in which an off-camera voice intoned, "It's not nice to fool Mother Nature." In the garden, you can't. Learning to live by nature's clock will, of necessity, teach patience and wonder and new ways of studying the world, in every season.

What can the human being do? To

A scheduling mix-up can be a stroke of good luck, if a gardener is flexible enough to take advantage of serendipity. *Below:* Photographer Walter Chandoha forgot to prune his ornamental grasses one autumn, only to discover that they looked good with his tulips the following spring. Now he deliberately plants bulbs where dried grasses will frame them.

begin with, you can learn to recognize the choices involved in creating, expanding, or rethinking your garden space.

Imagine a series of tissue overlays, each one detailing a particular issue of design or style; as you fill in each over-

lay and place it on the one before, your garden becomes more and more complex, expressive, personal. The next three chapters of this book present these choices—imaginary tissue overlays for you to consider. You can choose a garden that will pique and satisfy all five senses. You can choose the structure, literally and figuratively, that you want your garden to have. You can choose to give your garden a sense of space, of deliberate, sanctuary-like confinement, of organization, of destination. And only then will you choose the plants, not just for their texture and color, but also for how they grow (up, down, laterally) and how they work together.

As the gardens presented within these pages demonstrate, there are many ways to respect convention

Writer Sydney Eddison rightly calls winter the "unsung season." Designed around solid year-round sculpture—branches, fences, a shed—gardens like Lynden B. Miller's (left) look superb under the frostiest conditions. Flower colors may even distract from the beautiful contrasts of light and shadow.

without letting it restrict or control you. Some gardeners take convention and rumple it up; some take convention and twist it around. In any case, convention is merely the starting point—the same design principles used as starting points by different gardeners will take them to very different, very personal places. This is the element of style at work, and at play. The collection of real-life gardens gathered here is not meant to be templates to trace in their every detail, but rather models for reflecting various attitudes, moods, temperaments: style. Broken down into components for you to put together in order to create a garden uniquely your own.

"Only connect," E. M. Forster's gentle plea in *Howard's End,* can haunt you as much in the garden as elsewhere in this life. The garden connects us to a complex world, weaving its way through images in

Gardens nourish every part of our domestic lives, from discoveries shared with a wonder-struck child *(below)* to gatherings with friends *(opposite).*

our literature, adornments to our architecture, the thinking that goes into creating our public and private places, refrains in the work of artists whom we admire, and in history, legend, and lore.

Gardens also connect to other gardens, and gardeners. Our cities are much the better for the way our communities organize themselves around special-project gardens, community-tended greens, and the container plantings and window boxes that enhance our streets. Lawns are the connective tissue linking neighbors in our suburbs, but these lawns are changing. Take any street of houses that match, more or less. A few years ago, such a street would have had a sameness to it—outdoors. Only

Community gardens all across the country demonstrate the power of the land to bring diverse groups of people together. Boston's nine-acre Fenway Gardens *(above)* has been yielding bountiful harvests of goodwill since it was founded as a war-time Victory Garden in 1942.

indoors would you have been able to learn about the inhabitants, from their furniture, mementos, the books on the shelves, the art on the walls. Today, you can also learn about the inhabitants of each house through the gardens cropping up that alleviate the sameness. Increasingly, people are expressing who they are by what they plant.

To this writer, the garden has also assumed the role of muse. Anyone who writes must find subjects to write about that interest him or her personally, and I knew that, sooner or later, I wanted to write about gardening. That I was relatively new to the pursuit, and had—admittedly—limited experience didn't stop me, because I wanted to write a primer, for learn-as-you-go gardeners like me. Eventually I did, learning more as I wrote about certain steps that I'd always blithely skipped, such as amending the soil or applying the correct methods of pruning.

One of the wonderful things that came out of that project for me was having the chance to work with the editors of *Garden Design* magazine—an ongoing collaboration that led, eventually, to writing this book.

Every time I approach an assignment, I'm reminded that this magazine features gardens,

Despite municipally enforced maintenance standards and tacit pressure to conform, the lawn is slowly losing ground in suburbia. A California landscape of native plants and other drought-tolerant vegetation *(left)* designed by Schwartz and Associates of Sausalito, presents a lush yet frugal alternative to the neighbors' irrigated turf.

37

real people's gardens; by reading (and writing) their stories, I began to see how these gardeners gained their vision, so to speak, and how

The story of every new gardener is a profile in courage. Take the saga of Lisa Mierop, whose New Jersey property appears in these before-and-after photographs. When she decided to redo her backyard—then a jumble of spindly hemlocks and maples, and a scruffy lawn—Mierop didn't know an annual from a perennial. But she resolved to tear out everything and start from scratch. In preparation, she read garden books, studied catalogs, drew plans, and compiled plant lists.

their vision—and their gardens—changed over time. Sometimes I return to gardens I've already written about and am startled to find them transformed; inevitably, the gardener has had new ideas. That's the process, I came to understand. And that's the message of this book.

I never tire of interviewing people about their gardens, not only because every garden is different, but also because I believe that all gardeners, whether they're aware of it from the beginning or not, come to the pastime with a longing that they hope the garden will fill; I like eavesdropping on those longings. "This is the only place in the world where I can be creative," a Wall Street investment banker once told me, standing near an arc of tree peonies in full bloom that marked an edge of his border. "When I'm in the garden, it feels like my wife is still alive," said a grieving widower. Gardens also bring people into worlds that they never knew existed. Asked to research a story on daylilies, I fell into the arcane world of daylily hybridizers, got hooked, and never looked back. I met professionals and amateurs for whom these plants aren't a hobby, but a calling.

"It's the privacy I love," I've heard more than once, and it's true: gardens are private, intimate places, and gardens tell stories; gardeners are people who have learned to listen. To listen, and also to see: you view the world differently when you're looking at it with a gardener's eye. This book will give you that vision.

A backhoe made quick work of Mierop's yard, leaving her with a lot as barren as a moon crater *(opposite)* and a sinking feeling in her stomach. Still, her experience in interior design helped her visualize spaces and colors. To give the landscape dimension, she had the backhoe sculpt the soil. After five years of planting, digging up, and rearranging, Mierop's once drab yard is a luxuriant woodland garden *(below),* with hostas and ferns spilling over paths that meander past flowering shrubs. Every precious sunny spot overflows with flowers.

THE FIVE SENSES

2

sight

touch

smell

sound

taste

The fuzzy flower clusters, or panicles, of *Astilbe* are much more caressable than this perennial's common name, false goat's beard, might suggest. Held high above feathery leaves that also beg to be touched, the airy pink, red, salmon, or white plumes are surprisingly long-lasting, either in a partially shaded garden bed or indoors, as cut flowers in a vase.

I ONCE SAW a TV talk show in which ten women—large women, small women, of all ages— came onto the stage, each wearing a white T-shirt and khaki pants. The guest, a fashion designer, added scarves, belts, shoes, sweaters, blazers, vests, jewelry, you name it, to each of the women; by the end of the program, they all looked stylish and distinctive, as if dressed for ten separate occasions. You would never have noticed that they had started with the same blank sartorial slate.

Give ten different people pristine leather journals and ask them to keep a diary. In the end, you'll have ten voices, ten stories, all between the same two covers.

Visit the kitchens of ten great cooks. Same basic ingredients in all ten kitchens, same spices on the spice racks, same tools. After all the prep work, you'll sit down to ten unique and delicious meals that could range from scrambled eggs to a soufflé, all from the same starting point.

Or give ten gardeners free rein over say, a typical suburban-size plot of land. In the end, you'll have ten very different gardens.

There's no single right way to express yourself—in fashion, in words, in the kitchen, or in the garden, where, once you've followed certain fixed design principles (the "givens" of the garden; see Chapter 3, "The Essential Design Elements: Boundaries, Structures, Pathways, Water"), the rest is interpretation. How do you interpret nature? By a design strategy that draws together elements to tempt all the five senses. As you decide where you want your garden to be, the moods you want it to convey, and how you'll define and enclose it, you'll also want to determine from the earliest planning stages the ways you want your garden to look, feel, smell, sound, and taste.

A garden that exists solely to be admired at arm's length loses its appeal compared to gardens that are meant to be enjoyed and plunged into in every possible way. The sensual choices you make are personal; they make the garden your own, not some template you'll also find three houses down the street, and again over on the next block.

Sensual choices can convey a touch of whimsy, a visual joke, an element of aesthetic risk. Do you secretly yearn to combine deep reds, acid greens, and bright purples somewhere in your otherwise tasteful perennial border? Try it. Does the dangerous-looking hardy cockspur thorne, *Crataegus crus-galli*, suggest to you stark beauty, or pure Halloween? If you see drama in four-inch thorns, plant a specimen and watch it grow. Do you want your mint to taste like chocolate, lemon, apple—or plain old mint? Your call. Will your water rush, tumble, and splash, or simply reflect quietly? You get to decide your garden's sound system. Does boxwood, so pleasing in form, smell evocatively musky to you, or does it smell like stale kitty litter? Your choice: plant it where you can enjoy its fragrance, or its form. Always, the denser the sensual mix, the more compelling the garden, whether it's a closet-size terrace replete with every possible color and texture competing for space in pots, a grand-scale meadow with a distant view of the sea, or a backyard delineated with a stockade fence, all dark and green and punctuated with just one splash of color.

It is challenging, certainly, to sit at your desk with a pencil and a sheet of graph paper figuring out where paths and pergolas, beds and birdbaths, gates and gazebos will go, and then transform the sketch, all curves and crisp edges, from paper to the soil. But it's harder still to preconceive, let alone sketch in, sensations: the translucent aura that backlights ornamental grasses like a halo if you position each clump so that the sun will be directly behind it (at the optimum time of day for you to admire it); the scratch 'n' sniff magic that happens when you rub the leaf of a scented geranium and get a surprise hit of ginger or citrus; the quiet, methodical, hypnotic drip of water from a bamboo pipe (a noise, ironically, that would drive you crazy if it came from your bathroom faucet); the way moss muffles sound and intensifies the sense of cool retreat; the fusion of textures—rough, smooth, soft, prickly, fuzzy—that give a garden its tactile complexity; the sweetness you taste (real? imagined?) when you bite the tip of a honeysuckle blossom. This is the hidden design—the effects the senses create that help to give a garden its style.

How can you plan (and plant) for maximum sensory enjoyment? There's no precise design premise that will teach you; this is a lesson that comes from stretching the imagination. You don't learn it once. You learn it over and over as you go along, get to know your garden, fall in love with the way plants grow up, down, reach out, stretch toward the sun, refract the light. You learn it more as the confidence you feel in expressing other parts of your creative domestic life—how to make your house comfortable, where to place scented candles and paintings and bowls of fruit—takes hold outside. You begin to understand that you have the right to impose your ideas and aesthetics on nature.

You learn it more as the garden becomes not so much something to look at as a place to inhabit. You learn from the surprises the garden creates for you on its own, and from things you planned brilliantly, as well as from those that happen by accident. You have to see what happens,

Poke your nose into a fresh-picked bouquet of sweet basil, *Ocimum basilicum,* and inhale the essence of summer. It pays to plant more of this fast-growing annual herb than you expect to use in the kitchen—the aroma that is released when you brush against basil in the garden, or when the sun warms its leaves, is reason enough to have plenty around.

The squeak of shucked leaves starts us salivating over anticipated sweetness even before the kernels of 'Silver Queen' corn are laid bare. Because that sweetness begins to dull the instant an ear is picked, backyard farmers still find room for space-squandering cornstalks, and sprint from garden to stove (if they can resist nibbling the raw kernels).

what your plants tell you about how they look together, whether they're happy where you put them, whether their neighbors show them off to their best advantage. The art of expression in the garden (or anywhere else, for that matter) takes the science of design one step further. In a way, you plant all you know—from your reading, travels, friendships, your understanding of art, fashion, history, beauty, your sense of humor and willingness to experiment. A garden of the senses invites you to come all the way in.

Look at a lemon tree. Its shape is not exotic but familiar, oval on top, trunk on bottom, widest at the soil; it's in the sun, laden with golden fruit, a garden unto itself. What happens when you look? Your eyes water. Your mouth puckers. Your nose draws in the fragrance of a stray blossom. There's a delicate snap as you pluck off a fruit, making you wonder how it's possible that a lemon actually grew from so fragile a twig. And then you feel the heft and heat of the lemon in your hand. You've piqued all of the five senses. You've picked a miracle.

Think small in the garden, with miniature, contained theater pieces to study. Think big, as far as your eye can take you, to scenery you don't even own, to what Asians call "borrowed view." Look up: What have you silhouetted against the sky? Sit low to the ground: Do the underplantings smooth out the effects above? Study how the garden is reflected every which way in a mirror. Listen to the sounds you make as you walk—the padding of bare feet on brick, the crunch of boots on gravel—and the birds and bees and butterflies you gently interrupt as you pass by. Smell the garden morning, noon, and night. Touch the plants (sticky pine needles, self-explanatory lamb's ears, feathery nigella), and let them touch you. Feel the danger in a thorn that pricks, in bark that scratches your knuckles. Steep some applemint in hot, hot water and sip the tea you've grown. Use the senses as a checklist: Have you forgotten one? Can you layer some more? Have you set up surprises for visitors to discover and exclaim over? Do your solutions still compel you?

I've always liked the way judges of figure skating are asked to give two marks: one to evaluate the skater's technical performance and a second to judge the heart, soul, and verve of the performance—where the passion comes in. You can look at a garden and vote twice, too: How well is it designed and built technically? And how does it move and envelop you in sensual ways? A garden that may come up short in design but overflows with passion—and with all kinds of exuberant sensual life—will always be the hands-down favorite.

FRAME AND FOCUS Connoisseurs have been calling gardens "picturesque" since the eighteenth century, when views were carefully designed as 3-D counterparts of painted pictures—complete with foreground "frames" of trees, rocks, or buildings. This idea is still a useful way to plan a landscape with vantage points in mind, whether the frame is a window, a pair of shrubs, or a gateway, as here in the Connecticut garden of designer John Saladino.

sight

touch

smell

sound

taste

IN THE VILLAGE where I live, garden tours are an irresistible summer draw, offering the chance to peer behind closed garden gates and into other people's ideas. I once spent several days helping a friend prepare for her garden's public debut, a benefit tour scheduled for a late spring Saturday. On the Sunday before the event, the border looked spectacular; the petals of the Oriental poppies and tall late tulips, dozens of them, were spread as wide as they could be just before they'd begin to drop, one by one. Six more days, I thought to myself as we weeded, edged, and mulched—and silently implored those petals to hang in there. It was a stretch, thinking they'd make it until Saturday. It was Wednesday's rainstorm, targeting the tulips and toppling the poppies, that did us in. The garden looked the way I feel on a bad hair day, and we spent the next afternoon scurrying around like mad squirrels to the nurseries, filling in the bare spots so the garden would look perfect. As we left, my friend said to her garden: "Don't anything move."

That was the trouble, I thought, as we went from garden to garden, taking the tour ourselves. As in the children's game of statues, nothing moved. For years I looked at gardens in this way, from a garden-tourist's perspective, admiring the flowers only at their peak moments—"What a pretty drift!" (Gertrude Jekyll loved drifts)—before finally beginning to learn how to *see* a garden, which is a different matter entirely. In order to put a garden together, you have to be able to take it apart. You have to be analytical, in other words, before you can be sentimental. And that's how most of us get into trouble—we can't see the garden for the flowers.

When we're first drawn to gardening—and I've observed this enough to suspect that there's a developmental pattern at work here—many of us begin by admiring, learning about, and planting flowers. Then we begin to notice what flowers can't do (offer sculptural composition, suggest structure, frame a view, bloom perpetually, or anchor a bed year-round), and our preoccupation shifts, to shrubs and trees and how they can elevate the scale and complexity of a garden. In the next stage of development, we begin to see what the human being can do, and suddenly our new preoccupation is building: arbors, pergolas, gates, ornamental fences, and posts with plants to climb them. As our confidence increases, we want to garden bigger, literally rising to the challenge nature has offered us.

If I were starting over, the first lesson I would want to learn is how to understand vision in the largest, most expansive sense possible. From day one. You are the gardener, a human-scale reference point. Start on a majestic scale—a dozen times a day, every week, every month—looking straight up at the sky and then slowly down. Observe the vantage points, highlights, shadows, slopes, contours, the compositions that nature has already put into place. Start from the outside and work your way in: What do you need to frame? What do you need to hide? What do you want to adorn? What should you create from scratch? So much of why a garden works is due to the way we ourselves see, and so much of why gardeners are forever changing things around is our endless capacity for learning to see better. Beyond the flowers, into the garden, and back.

BORROWED VIEW
The smaller the garden, the more it benefits from an ancient Asian design strategy (*jie jing* in China, *shakkei* in Japan), borrowing views—the artful framing of scenery outside the garden that makes the property appear to stretch beyond its boundaries. Here, in the Pacific Northwest, trees have been thinned to "borrow" mountains as a backdrop for the owner's shrubs.

WAYS 5 TO LOOK AT A GARDEN

Light colors (such as yellow and white) tend to advance, dark colors (blue, purple) to recede. If you want to make a shallow bed or border seem deeper, **put dark-toned foliage and flowers toward the back** and bright foliage and flowers up front.

To evaluate plantings for foliage texture and silhouette, **take black-and-white photos,** not color.

To make a straight path or an allée seem longer, **taper the sidelines toward a central "vanishing point."** To enhance the illusion, plant flanking trees of different heights, graduating from tall in the foreground to short in the distance.

Gauge light the way your sun- or shade-loving plants do, by plotting the course of the sun on the ground over time. **Track shadows cast by trees or buildings** using stakes to mark their limits at sunup, noon, and sundown throughout the year.

For a moonlight garden, **plant white varieties of fast-growing annuals**: *Nicotiana sylvestris,* cosmos, alyssum, cleome, sunflowers, impatiens, zinnias, moonflowers, and petunias.

SILHOUETTE It is easy to be seduced by the brilliant colors and textures of plants in full daylight and to forget the patterns they create when the sun is behind them. Whether positioning flowers, grasses, or trees (like these on a Michigan estate by the midwestern master Jens Jensen), plan for dramatic silhouettes.

SMALL WORLD

The gardener with a tight corner to tend can use the same tricks of scale that turn a model train set into a transcontinental railroad or let a five-inch bonsai tree in a dish conjure up a forest sequoia. In this 336-square-foot Oregon courtyard, designed by William Cunningham and Pat Lando of Creative Gardens in Portland, a few large rocks suggest mountains, lichens look like copses, and water trickling from a recirculating pump becomes a virtual river.

REFLECTION
A mirror hung at the back of
a shaded arbor, or set within
the frame of a false exterior
window or doorway, brings light
into dark recesses and creates
the illusion of a looking-glass
landscape beyond a blank wall.
Similar sleight of hand can be
achieved more elaborately with
trompe l'oeil paintings, like
the ancient garden vistas that
survive on villa walls in Pompeii.

CLOSE-UP

In gardens, as on film, close-ups combine breathtaking intimacy with insight into character. Every season gives fresh cause for getting up close and personal with plants. *Opposite:* Autumn offers seed heads like this halo of *Tragopogon pratensis*. *Left:* Scarlet veins of Swiss chard pulse with summer heat.

55

SIGHT GAG The role of humor as a traditional element of garden design is often overlooked. There's the ribaldry of oversexed statuary satyrs, as well as the practical jokes of Renaissance princelings, who hid lackeys behind the shrubbery to open secret valves that drenched unsuspecting guests. But there is also the wit of this clipped-yew rider and hounds at Ladew Topiary Gardens, deep in Maryland's hunt country.

BACKLIGHTING

Vivid autumn foliage, like the leaves of this Japanese maple, takes on a jewel-like brilliance when it is seen with the rising or setting sun shining through. The linear patterns of branches, leaf veins, and fence slats intensify the glow, like the leading in a stained glass window.

sight

touch

smell

sound

taste

IT'S ALL WELL AND GOOD to touch the petal of a rose and feel its miraculous soft-ness, but that's the payoff at the end of a lot of other touching, most of it neither miraculous nor soft. How do you create a garden in the first place? By undoing what nature has already done, starting over. In most cases, long before you get to touch a rose petal, you'll be trying to root out endless underground runners, fat as hoses, that seem to connect to nothing. You'll be untangling things with brambles, thistles, and thorns, and pulling up weeds, tugging at unwanted clumps of grass, and turning over unsuitable soil. The garden is no place for the weak or faint-hearted. You'll find yourself putting Band-Aids on nicks and scratches, salve on the sunburn you didn't mean to get, and lotion on the rash from the poison ivy you failed to notice.

And you'll be handling tools, perfectly weighted for their tasks and unchanged, basically, from tools used centuries ago for the same purposes. You'll be hefting bales of peat, pushing wheelbarrows full of compost, toting bags of manure. You'll be in touch with the earth and the sun in a way that strains your muscles, clears your head, and makes you feel hungry, thirsty, and sweaty—exhilarating and primal sensations, so different from the genteel appetite occasioned by a polite game of tennis or a bike ride to town.

Gloves or no gloves? You can learn so much from what your fingers tell you about the diverse textures of leaves, stems, buds, and blossoms, about the intricate ways smooth roots map themselves into ever-smaller water- and nourishment-seeking tributaries, about the feel of the soil. These sensations are the essential tactile correlatives to what your eye tells you. There's nothing like the feeling of working warm, friable soil with your fingertips. Or, you can break in suede or goatskin gloves until they soften and conform to your hand like a second but protec-tive skin. Instinct will guide you when you begin to handle plants themselves, using your fork to loosen the roots of, say, a hosta tightly bound in its pot, or using unfamiliar muscles to cajole a heavy clump of *Fargesia* bamboo, burlap-tied roots and all, into the hole you've dug. You'll feel like a big, gritty mess, and you'll probably also feel pretty happy at the same time.

After you've touched the garden in all these ways, the garden will begin to touch you back; you'll feel it beckoning. Plants will brush against you as you walk along a path you've laid or enter a door you've framed. They'll stretch toward you, grow closer to one another, and, as they do, begin to fill in the empty spaces around them with color, texture, and shadow. The boundaries of the garden will start to smudge, as your graph-paper plan takes on a life of its own. Now it's your turn to handle again—to prune, pinch, deadhead, stake, tie up, cut down.

And do all the touching you want. As children, we're taught not to walk on the grass, not to pick the flowers, to approach the garden as if a velvet cord kept us at a respectful distance. It's a hard lesson to unlearn, but in order to really know a garden, you have to touch it, gather it in—fill and claim and study your space with your physical presence. And only then stop to touch the miraculous softness of that rose petal.

SHAGGY BARK

As children, we are taught to
value trees for blossom and leaf;
regrettably, our schooling usually
stops short of bark appreciation. But
a glorious paperbark maple, *Acer
griseum*, opens our eyes—and draws
our fingers—to the tangible delight
a trunk can give long after the fall.

PATINA

Just as verdigris on an
ancient bronze idol enhances
its allure, so the lichens that
mottle a weathered rock
endow a garden with rugged,
venerable beauty. It's worth
the wait to let nature supply
the patina of moss that
blunts the sharp edges of
new hardscaping and
marries it to the land.

Garden **surfaces for
bare feet:** sun-warmed
bluestone paving, cool,
well-worn clay paths, silky
fescue lawns, a matted carpet of woolly thyme.

At times **our fingers see
better than our eyes:**
seeking a soft, ripe tomato
hidden in foliage; prying
loose wiry roots of
quackgrass interlaced
through soft soil.

It's tempting to feel the
warm soil and tender leaves
and tiny roots with bare fingertips, and yet there is no
surer way of drying and
cracking skin. **Gloves are
the answer,** though cotton,
suede, and rubber can all
seem annoyingly bulky.
Goatskin gloves, however,
are soft and supple, even
retaining the shape of your
hands. Wash the gloves with
kitchen soap while you are
wearing them; then lay
them out to dry.

Most huggable trees:
American beech, with dry,
skin-textured bark;
sycamore (the light-and-
dark peeling bark looks like
giraffe hide); sequoia, for a
big squeeze.

In addition to cuddly lamb's
ears, **plants that ask to be
grasped** include: the grasses
Miscanthus and *Pennisetum*,
all ferns, and *Mimosa pudica,*
or sensitive plant, which folds
up shyly afterward.

Perennial *Physostegia
virginiana* is said to have
received its common name,
obedient plant, because its
small, spiky flowerheads
tend to remain angled
wherever you bend them.

FUZZ

Lamb's ears, as *Stachys byzantina*
is fittingly known, ranks high in most
gardeners' lists of lovable fuzzies.
Children can't keep their hands
off it (try the family-size, fungus-
resistant cultivar 'Big Ears'). The
name pinpoints the appeal of woolly
foliage: besides making the smooth,
glossy leaves of border companions
seem sleeker by contrast, a soft pelt
almost turns a plant into a pet.

PRICKLY SPINES

In the garden, an element
of danger can be thrilling,
so long as nobody gets hurt.
The don't-touch-me glamour
of spiny succulents like this
cactus, *Parodia magnifica*,
creates surefire drama
in warm, dry climates. Spiky
agave and thorny trifoliate
orange, *Poncirus trifoliata*,
are deliciously menacing
too; just make sure that
paths are broad enough
to prevent uncomfortably
close encounters.

FLUFF

Let go to seed, ornamental grasses (like two-foot-tall *Pennisetum alopecuroides* 'Hameln', below) raise downy tassels that dance in the slightest breeze or quiver at the flick of a fingertip. When most garden flowers dwindle in fall, the grasses' airy bouquets still wave, lasting well into winter.

BRUSHING UP

There is more than a trace of Tarzan or Jane in many gardeners' romance with the land. Such adventurers crave paths where you can't walk two paces without being tapped by a frond overhead or stroked by a leaf at your side. In San Francisco garden designer Sonny Garcia's jungly domain, left, intrepid visitors begin their trek down the path by wading through a clump of variegated grasses.

63

sight

touch

sound

taste

smell

LAST SPRING, SHORTLY after my daughter Jenna's first birthday, when she was just beginning to toddle, we visited friends and took a walk through their woodland garden, along a path lined with fragrant daffodils that were precisely the height of her nose. From where I stood, taller, they seemed to stretch into the woods forever. The trees, rising above us like giant sculptures, didn't have leaves yet; the daffodils were the show—show and smell. Jenna stopped to sniff every daffodil she could, exclaiming each time. Throughout the summer, whenever she spotted a nose-high display of any kind, she'd run off to sniff it, and I always felt a pang of regret when I knew in advance that those plants were scentless and would disappoint her.

Lilacs, daphnes, lily of the valley, sweet woodruff, peonies, lilies, and daylilies were a great success, while she disdained lavender, rosemary, and yarrow—probably too musky. At a nursery, Jenna zeroed in on pots of "Scentunias," new hybrid petunias bred for their unbelievably sweet aroma, and I bought one to hang by the side door so she could smell it deeply every day on her way in and out. (I confess to having been a snob about petunias up until then, but the scent drifting in all summer was lovely.) She loved honeysuckle (especially *Lonicera periclymenum* 'Graham Thomas'), Korean spice (*Viburnum carlesii*), a scented mock orange (*Philadelphus coronarius* 'Aureus'), and a *Vitex vagnus-castus* I tracked down at friends' houses. One night, she got to stay up late at a friend's "nighttime" garden, where the scents of nicotiana, moonflowers, and angel's trumpets didn't release themselves until past her usual bedtime. She turned away from an overpoweringly fragrant rose garden the way I reacted to a great-aunt of mine, whose liberal use of talcum powder and violet water, I think it was, always made me hold my breath. "Too much," Jenna seemed to want to say, as she fled to the sidelines to sniff from afar.

In the perfume business, the "top note" is the smell of the fragrance when it's initially applied, before it settles into what's known as the "heart" scent and then descends to the "dry-down," the subtle echo that lingers for hours. In the garden, fragrant plants are all top note. So design for scent where you want it—at your garden's pulse points: near doorways and windows, where you sit, where you walk, where you walk to. Or where you dine alfresco. The delicious smell of food wafting from the kitchen or the grill is heady, but too many fragrances competing for one nose can detract from the one you want to dominate: the scent of dinner.

You read all your life about *perfumed this* and *perfumed that*, but fragrance must be experienced in person. Your imagination can't lead you to a scent, nor can your memory, although the reverse is true; scent is a rich physical connector. A remembered fragrance (the aroma of Gauloises taking you back to student days in Paris, the smell of a pine-rimmed lake evoking summer camps) can resuscitate a memory. Coming upon smell unexpectedly in a garden is thrilling. It took a June evening (perfect conditions: cool, slightly damp, light breeze) on a porch under late-blooming white wisteria, so fragrant I felt I'd carry away the scent, for me to understand that fragrance isn't just a bonus or afterthought in the garden—it's something worth planning for all along.

CLASSIC ROSE
Some roses are redolent of
cloves (*Rosa* 'Belle Poitevine')
and some have the scent of tea
(*R.* 'Duchesse de Brabant'); some
are overwhelmingly perfumed
(*R.* 'Dolly Parton') and some are
practically odorless (*R.* 'The Fairy');
some, such as *R.* 'Eden Rose 88'
(*above*), just smell like a perfect rose.

PINEY WOODS

You needn't hike through the forest to enjoy the keen, bracing fragrance of pine (forget the fake-balsam reek of namesake air fresheners). From the moment you plant one pine tree in your yard, you can release Mother Nature's incense by gently rubbing a needle between two fingers. For a full-strength blast to the nostrils, snip a stem.

HEADY HYACINTH

In the spring garden, the potent sweetness of hyacinth flowers stops you in your tracks. In a living room where the windows are shut, a few cut hyacinth blooms or a single potted bulb can almost knock you out with their cloying intensity. Still, like inhaling an early narcissus or lilac, a whiff of hyacinth is a hallowed rite of spring.

AROMATIC HERBS

As pungently perfumed as it is colorful, lavender was brought to North America by European settlers, who wove it into patterned herb beds like this modern knot garden at Filoli, near San Francisco. Since the seventeenth century, dried lavender florets, which retain their scent for up to three years, have been added to jellies and wine, bathwater and linen sachets.

7 WAYS TO BE LED BY THE NOSE

Many of the finest floral **fragrances emerge at dusk,** to lure night-flying pollinators. Top prospects for moonlit gardens: datura, brugmansia, stocks, moonflower vine, cactus, magnolia, four o'clocks, petunias, and nicotiana.

Trees and shrubs that **perfume an entire garden:** *Magnolia grandiflora*, crab apple, lilac, citrus gardenia, *Eucalyptus melliodora*, linden, mock orange (*Philadelphus*), *Elaeagnus pungens,* acacia, *Paulownia*. Trees that stink up the joint: chestnut, pear, hawthorn, ginkgo.

Most fragrant fruit: strawberry, ripe muskmelon, and quince.

For floral scents **outdoors in late winter** and early spring, plant witch hazel, wintersweet, daphne, and the honeysuckle *Lonicera fragrantissima.*

Herbs with varieties in multiple fragrances: mint (chocolate, lemon, apple, pineapple) and scented geranium, *Pelargonium* (lemon, peppermint, orange, rose, nutmeg, cinnamon, and almond).

Plant miniature creeping thymes along the sides of paths and between pavers, to **release scent as you walk** or sit among them.

For a hint of **cherry blended with honey,** plant heliotrope; for the sweetest **cinnamon,** plant carnations and pinks (both *Dianthus*); for **chocolate,** *Cosmos atrosanguineus.*

WHISPERS

If wind and water provide the garden's subtlest background music, the whitest noise of all is the murmur of fine grasses. At John Greenlee's California nursery, on the coast near Malibu, Mexican feather grass, *Stipa tenuissima*, catches the breeze.

sound

WHAT IF PLANTS had a native tongue, and that tongue were English? What if nature had given every creature in the garden, from ladybugs to hummingbirds to voles, a huge booming voice? Can you imagine the racket? When you consider the bounty of life the garden nurtures and sustains, it's amazing that you have to listen so carefully to hear it.

Arguably the subtlest of the garden's sensual pleasures, sound nonetheless imparts a curiously intimate dimension to the way you experience a landscape. From spending time alone outside, any gardener can call up certain sounds from memory: the crunch of the earth when you turn it with a spade; the muffled, crumbly sound that compost makes when you spread it; the neat staccato snapping that begins to repeat itself when your pruning takes on a hypnotic rhythm of its own; the "thwunk" that reverberates straight down into the immovable earth when you let a shrub in a heavy pot fall onto the ground before planting it. Then there are the sounds the gardener himself makes—groans and grunts and quick expulsions of breath after heaving, stretching, and lifting—the pleasing and honest sounds of unforced labor.

When you invite others into the garden, the sounds are different; if sounds were light, they would cast varying shades and shadows, depending on the time of day. When the light is morning-clear, for example, there's a crispness to the sound of breakfast outdoors against the silence of the garden, entirely unlike the energetic morning clatter of a breakfast room. At lunch, with the light filtered through the haze of high noon, voices don't hit the walls and bounce back, the way they do in a dining room. Instead, they float off, like languid balloons, high above the garden walls, leaving time somehow suspended in their wake. In the evening, voices in the garden reverberate like the ring of crystal, nothing like the way voices blur at a dinner party indoors. In the garden, even the sound of children changes. Muffled, perhaps, by layers of plants, the voices of children playing on a brick terrace have softer edges than those same voices carrying across an asphalt playground. Add a cascade, or even a trickle, of water, and all of those sounds will persist in your memory.

City dwellers arriving for a country visit invariably complain of how noisy the quiet is; the background sounds of the garden come with the territory. Bees buzzing, birds swooping and calling, dry leaves crackling underfoot in the autumn, the crunch of gravel: the sounds of arrival, departure, convergence. You never think about "planting" sound outdoors, but the more you build and furnish the garden and deliberately choose and position the plants and give them time to settle in, the more the sound of a garden comes to life. Put in some silvery feather grass, *Stipa pennata*, for example, and you'll magnify the whistle of any breeze. It will whisper in light wind, and it'll thunder in a storm. Add a stone terrace or a wooden deck, and the sounds of footsteps will change; add voices and you'll alter the echoes. Install birdhouses and bird feeders, and you'll encourage more birdsong. Tie some wind chimes to a tree, on the other hand, and you may risk going too far. You may drown out the wind.

RUSTLING

Don't be in such a rush to rake and bag every last autumn leaf. Crushed underfoot, this seasonal windfall isn't only the makings of good mulch; it's also the essential snap, crackle, and pop for a walk in the woods—or the little glade you've dubbed a woodland garden. Even kids who couldn't care less about birdcalls or wind chimes will remember this crunch decades from now with Proustian nostalgia.

MUFFLED FOOTSTEPS

What's more luxurious than the silent padding of bare feet on moss? This natural carpet flourishes in the worst conditions—damp shade and poor acid soil—but it takes patience to start a moss garden (like this one at Kenilworth, in Asheville, North Carolina) from scratch. After clearing weeds from the site, get permission to dig a bit from a friend's lawn (moss isn't readily available in the nursery trade). Then mix a handful of moss with a cup of buttermilk in a blender, and spread it about. Weed and water regularly for the first two years. This is one place where you'll need to rake or blow fallen leaves, because they may smother the moss.

6 SOUNDS WORTH LISTENING FOR

Dawn and dusk are the best times to weed, not just because the air is cooler, but also because **the calling of birds is richest then.**

You will **hear a hummingbird's wings** minutes before you'll catch sight of the elusive little creature. To create an attractive habitat, plant red impatiens, salvias, and cardinal climber.

Consider plants as wind instruments. Position any conifer—pine, spruce, or hemlock—outside a bedroom window: the wind sighing through the **needled branches will lull you to sleep.** A clump of the tall grass *Miscanthus* also murmurs a lullaby nearly year-round. Late in fall, seedpods of *Baptisia* **rattle cheerfully.** A beech hedge is soothing all winter, as breezes make the dry, longlasting copper leaves hiss like the surf.

On a hot summer day you sometimes hear **mysterious insectlike popping sounds** emitted by plants, such as *Euphorbia palustris*, as they blast tiny seed over the garden.

Install a fountain; even a tiny one will work magic. The sound of moving water—splashing, trilling, bubbling, frothing—has **the power to muffle intrusive noise** that far exceeds its own volume.

Roses that **blessedly remain silent:** 'Big Ben', 'Banshee', 'Disco', 'Elvis', 'Surfer Girl', 'Tom Tom'.

BIRDSONG
The more varied your plantings
—flowers, shrubs, conifers, and
deciduous trees—the likelier you
are to host a year-round avian
music festival. Gardens help
replace natural habitats lost to
the development of wild land,
as well as supply the berries, seeds,
insects, and other delicacies that
tempt birds to sing for their supper.

WATER MUSIC Be it the tranquil monotone of a bamboo flume dripping into a Shinto stone basin or the roar of a Baroque fountain, liquid refreshment turns any landscape into an oasis. Even barely audible splashing distracts us from traffic noise and other nuisances. The bamboo pipe in the Japanese garden was designed to audibly click as water flowed through it to frighten deer and other night wildlife. Today, it is often secured to avoid the click, which some find annoying.

taste

ASK ANY FORMER schoolkid where agriculture began and you'll get the facts: Mesopotamia. The Fertile Crescent, the plain between the Tigris and the Euphrates. What else? Um, very fertile, there in the Fertile Crescent. I never stopped to wonder back then, in the dry history lessons of the fifth grade, what those gardens in the Fertile Crescent looked like, where the plants came from (no seed catalogs? no nurseries?), what people had grown to eat. Had the Sumerians discovered that rosemary is a splendid accompaniment to lamb? Did they already know about zucchini? Who figured out that tiny end-of-season fennel seeds are pungent palate cleansers? And which sorry fellow learned the hard way that monkshood is deadly poisonous?

In fact, there were marshes between the two rivers, and at first, all that grew there were unpalatable twenty-five-foot-tall reeds called *Phragmites australis*. Around 3000 B.C., the Sumerians drained the marshes into canals, setting up systems to irrigate the drier but fertile plains nearby. They planted fruits and vegetables, as well as a few ornamentals, though we're not sure what. Fast-forward to the 1960s, when all vegetables seemed to come shrink-wrapped or frozen, and you can see why, to schoolchildren of that era, the Fertile Crescent was less than exciting. Jump ahead a few decades more, to the availability of fresh herbs and vegetables year-round. Now, with a newfound lust for flavor, we're learning how to taste the garden. Maybe it's not coincidental that our rising culinary standards accompany a new appreciation of what the land can do.

I remember how skeptical I was the first time a friend offered me a nasturtium leaf to nibble: How did I know it was safe—or good—to eat? But the flat peppery leaf was the freshest thing I'd ever tasted. And it inspired me to grow other things for my tastebuds: 'Sweet 100' cherry tomatoes and Alpine strawberries; sour sorrel; even bitter arugula. Today, one of my greatest pleasures is going out to my herb garden with a pair of scissors. Even in late November, I can cut huge bouquets of sage (I lay them over quartered Spanish onions, which have been tossed in oil, balsamic vinegar, salt, and pepper, and roast them at 325 degrees for two hours). Or I can raid my friend's vegetable patch for the last of the squashes and find a lone eggplant for home-grown ratatouille. Growing, cooking, eating—one of life's simplest, purest cycles.

To celebrate the sense of taste, you don't need a full-fledged potager (the French word for "kitchen garden"), unless you want one. I regret that nurseries put perennials in one place, annuals in another, herbs somewhere else, arranging plant "categories" as an either/or proposition instead of how they work together best. A few beautiful edibles can enhance a purely ornamental garden. And some will argue that edibles *are* purely ornamental: consider pear trees espaliered against a wall. It may be unconventional to grow pumpkins among the perennials, but I love mixing feathery fennel with thalictrum, or perennial salvia with mysterious borage. Golden creeping thyme makes a tasty, front-of-the-border ground cover, lollipop alliums bloom with the late tulips, rampant mint looks surprisingly pretty among Siberian irises, and a graceful spray of lemongrass can be the centerpiece of a bed of disheveled annuals like cosmos. Mixed metaphors? Maybe. But just as friends like to hang out in the kitchen; even better is grazing in the garden.

JUST PICKED
Bored with the bland, mushy
blueberries at the supermarket?
Grow a plump, toothsome crop
of your own. The highbush
blueberry, *Vaccinium corymbosum*,
shown here, and Southern
rabbiteye blueberry, *V. ashei*,
are two of the tastiest.

FRESH-CUT Herbs newly harvested from the garden or from windowsill planters have incomparable depth and complexity of flavor. The thyme, basil, and rosemary on this cutting board are basic ingredients for the well-stocked kitchen garden.

SUN-RIPENED

Many a flower gardener happily heads to the farm stand or green-grocer for every kind of produce but one: tomatoes. None are quite so good as the ones you raise at home. Vermont seedsman Shepherd Ogden, who grows more than sixty varieties, praises the taste of this 'Red Currant' as "Exceptional."

8 WAYS TO PLEASE YOUR PALATE

Sunshine is **the secret to sweetness.** Virtually all vegetables will taste best harvested in the evening, after a full day in the sun.

To sweeten cool-weather vegetables often thought of as bitter—kale, collards, broccoli, Brussels sprouts—**expose them to frost** before picking and cook them (within a few hours of harvest) until barely wilted.

The buds of daylily, *Hemerocallis,* are **a treasured vegetable in Asia.** Yellow-flowered varieties taste best.

The **blossoms of virtually any culinary herb**—rosemary, basil, mustard, chives, and the multitude of salvias—are edible and provide a milder version of the same plant's leaf flavors.

Apples with a pleasing **hint of anise:** 'Freyburg', 'Blushing Golden', 'Yellow Delicious'.

Best **heirloom tomatoes** —richest: 'Brandywine', 'Suddeth's Brandywine'; for cooking: 'Early Large Red'; yellow: 'Golden Queen', 'Golden Ruffles'; frost-tolerant: 'Shenandoah'; delicate: 'White Queen'; biggest: 'Radiator Charlie's Mortgage Lifter'.

The **hottest peppers:** varieties of ají, cayenne, chiltepín, habanero, and Thai.

Rediscover the delicate flavor of **wild strawberries** by planting alpine varieties as edging in flower beds.

DELICATE
The garden pea,
Pisum sativum, has
been tempting
refined palates since
it graced the table
of Louis XIV. If
springtime has a
taste, it's the crisp,
exquisitely earthy
flavor of this cool-
weather marvel.

VOLUPTUOUS

Reaching up to pluck a ripe fig and savoring its honeyed pulp is about as sensuous as gardening gets (unless you prefer leaving fruit on the tree to turn even more sugary as it dries). This exotic indulgence is easier to cultivate in North America than many gardeners imagine. Native to Mediterranean regions, figs are hardy in **USDA** zones 8 to 10 (see zone map, page 303), though some varieties may thrive in zone 7 if planted against a south-facing wall or in a sheltered area.

THE ESSENTIAL DESIGN ELEMENTS

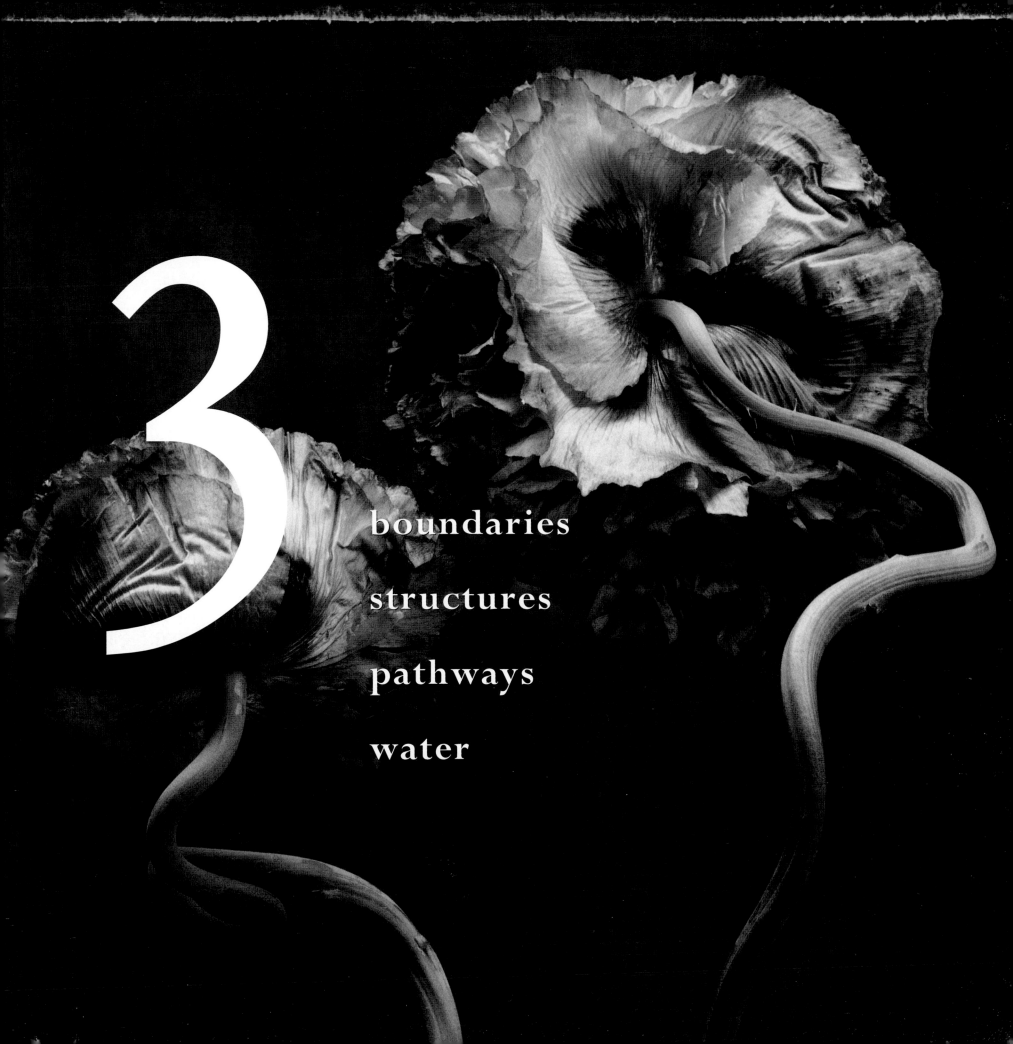

3 boundaries

structures

pathways

water

MY HUSBAND AND I bought our first house just a couple of years ago, a clunky place that needed (still needs) plenty of improvement. Michael's first big idea—which I vetoed—was to build a tower right in the middle of the roof so that he could climb up and look all around, maybe even see the water that's tantalizingly out of our visual reach, beyond some uninviting woods.

My idea was to start the garden with a pergola.

After having tended one garden, and planted another, my interest now was in really designing one, defining the space, making it clear that the garden wasn't just pretty flowers and shrubs, but a place with a clear-cut structural logic, a garden that flowed from one area, one mood, to another and guided a visitor through it, the way a good plot leads a reader through a novel. Space, any space, is chaos. This time I really wanted to order it.

The best parallel I can think of is of two lofts I've visited in New York City. In the first, the space is amorphous—a sofa and chairs over here, a dining table over there, a bed and dresser in the farthest corner, a makeshift office in the middle. You have to imagine the boundaries, and I feel oddly lost there, as if I can never figure out where I am or what I'm supposed to be doing. The second loft is different. The living room is partitioned with bookcases, which also form a wall for the dining area, and each of the spaces is painted a different color and further defined by carpets on the wood floors. The kitchen is laid out with a tile floor, and the sleek steely back of an industrial stove, hood attached, serves as another partial wall; the bedroom "walls" are screens. Each space is set off and self-contained—but you can still glimpse each space from the others. Even though it's a big, raw loft, with pipes running fully visible around the ceiling, it's the coziest place imaginable. I always feel at home there, safe somehow. My urge was to define the raw space in our new garden in the same orderly way. Which is why I wanted a pergola.

My eventual wish list included all kinds of outdoor spaces (a formal herb garden, a front courtyard affair, a meandering path with grasses alongside, and on and on), but my immediate concern was the garden we would live in, which rolled directly out of the back of the house. There was a stockade fence at the property line, and a big expanse of brick terrace outside the kitchen and dining-room doors. The garden that we would see from much of the house would be between the terrace and the fence. The pergola I envisioned would be to the left of the terrace facing the back of the house and connecting with the house itself, serving almost as a protective embrace to enclose

The simple yet
powerful geometry of
paths, gateways, and
raised beds tames
exuberant plantings
at Montrose, Nancy
Goodwin's North
Carolina garden.

No fair-weather friend, the concrete cherub in Christin Gangi's New Jersey backyard is as congenial in winter, looking down on snow-covered beds, as it is here, in summer, minding the gardener's gloves in a thicket of fennel.

the area. It would bring the scale of the two-story house down to a more human level and, with its far side trellised, give us some privacy from the neighbors' pool. There would be a doorway in the trellis, too, to suggest a flow to (eventual) gardens beyond. Wisteria would cover it quickly, and create a real room, a shelter for dining or sitting in the shade. And the whole garden could (eventually) emanate every which way from this structure.

It must be a primal need to stake out land, blaze a trail, claim a space by imposing the human will (and taste) on the natural landscape. Since the beginning of time, successful gardens have reconciled and harmonized two essential questions: What can man do? and What can nature do? The legendary Hanging Gardens of Babylon didn't just hang, for example. They climbed up things and spilled over terraces fortified by ornamental rock walls. Persian gardens, models for the paradise of the medieval imagination, were walled, literally. Ancient Roman gardens were elaborately constructed with colonnades and geometric paths; Renaissance Italians expanded that idea with vine-covered pergolas and labyrinths of clipped trees. As for the French in the time of Louis XIV, sometimes they hardly bothered with plants. Many a bed in their "embroidered" formal landscapes was neatly filled in with colored sand, gravel, or chipped stone. There isn't an historic legacy or aesthetic that doesn't send us principles for designing gardens today: shape the space. Figure out ways to move through the space. Create garden rooms. Embellish them. Make them your own.

What it boils down to is framing nature, carving it out, building structures or imposing elements that will fix the garden in its space, then letting the plants fill in the frames, growing in them, up them, over them, around them, against them. How? It is all up to you. This chapter presents an array of possibilities—arbors and arches, hedges and fences, ponds and pools—that will help you choose which elements will anchor your garden, and begin to tell its story.

Are there limitations? Sure. The space, the soil, the sun, the shade, the gradation of the land, the look of the house, the views beyond it, time, and money, among others; the limitations are the challenges. But the garden thrives as a harmonious truce between human and horticultural imprints on the land. The boundaries, the pathways, the structures you choose are the elements that show nature to its best effect—and make sense of it for human inhabitants.

The first spring, all I planted was wisteria, to climb the pergola with which we put our first mark on the land.

boundaries

picket fencesgateshedgesretaining wallsespaliersshrub borderstrelliseslatticeworkha-hasfieldstone wallssplit-rail

THE IMPULSE to shape space—to enclose it, to open it up, to keep things in, keep things out—must be as old as the basic sense of self-preservation. With garden boundaries, we plant or build them not to ward off plunderers, but to provide privacy, to give the eye (and the soul) the security that comes from knowing that you're in a protected place, that the space has been mapped out, that this territory is where you're meant to be.

There are other reasons. You might plant a hedge or build a wall as a barricade, to shelter other plants against a harsh wind or to make it possible to grow things a little less hardy. You might use a hedge or a wall to create smaller garden rooms within larger ones; it's amazing the way even a low wall or hedge can etch out a space. If you have a pool, you might need a fence by law, and want to make it an architectural feature of the larger garden. Or perhaps you have plunderers, as I do: deer. (One of the weirdest hedges I've ever seen is my own, behind a fence on one side of the house, a lineup of a dozen *Poncirus trifoliata*, an exotic member of the citrus family, with truly sinister thorns. It's dramatic as a specimen or grown in a pot. As a hedge—it's pure Addams Family. But it works, at least for that particular section of fence.)

Because boundaries, constructed or planted, are architectural features, they suggest moods—the formality of a high brick wall, the coziness of a picket fence, the difference between a hedge low enough to talk to your neighbors over and one as high and lush as a ballroom. How do you choose? By considering what's outside the boundary: is it something you want to see, or something you don't? By considering what's inside the boundary and how you wish to frame it. By practical concerns, like the ready availability of materials, how to match boundary to house, the budget, and, in the case of a hedge—time. How long are you willing to wait for this privacy and protection? And, of course, by sentimental concerns, such as whether all your life you've dreamed of a mending wall.

SHELTERING WALLS
Letting nature in, as well as keeping it out, cinder-block walls around May Moir's Hawaiian garden do double duty for her beds of bromeliads, tender members of the pineapple family. Many of the blocks have been turned on their sides, exposing their hollow cores, to admit the gentle trade winds that bromeliads need to flourish. At the same time, the expanse of masonry is a buffer against harmful, stronger winds.

FENCE AS TRANSITION
Enveloped by trumpet vine,
Dale Booher and Lisa Stamm's
Long Island gateway *(left)* is a
happy marriage of horticulture
and architecture. Painting
the cutout fence the deep
green of summer leaves
strengthens that connection,
much as the gate joins
different areas of the garden.

FENCE AS DEFINITION
There's no blurring of boundary
lines in Judith Jahnke's simple,
though unmistakably geometric,
garden enclosure near
Charlottesville, Virginia *(right)*.
Picket fences divide two spaces
and two moods: vegetable
beds softened by flowers
inside, and cottagey borders
with daisies and foxgloves in
bloom outside. The decision
to coat the fence in crisp
white paint was key: think
how different, how much more
rustic, the garden would look
if the fence had been left to
weather to a muted gray. In
white, the pickets stand out as a
dazzling backdrop against which
flowers and foliage can shine.

boundaries

As they grow, hedges define an outdoor room as effectively as solid walls, if not so quickly (it took decades for Barbara Chevalier's looming cypresses in Stinson Beach, California to reach 22 feet). The relative smallness of the doorway cut through this enclosure gives the room all the more majesty, though a planted alcove with a low boxwood hedge around an apple tree assert a more domestic scale. If this were an indoor room, the box hedge would be a wainscot or chair rail. Even a knee-high hedge shapes space with authority.

HEDGES

Clipped hedge. When you plant a wall for privacy, protection, or to enclose a space, you're doing exactly what ancient Roman gardeners did, and what gardeners have been doing ever since. When you use a single kind of plant that's either dense and regular in its growth habit (like hornbeam) or easily clipped into an unbroken mass (boxwood, privet, or yew, for example), the hedge will be stately and formal, whatever its height. Vary the uniformity by carving doors, windows, or niches. A miniature hedge of box, santolina, germander, or other shrubs and herbs with dense foliage is the classic outline for an herb garden or parterre.

Naturalistic hedge. A less formal way to partition space, while still using one kind of plant for consistent color and texture, is to create an informal lineup of shrubs or trees that isn't clipped to rigid attention. Instead, plants are allowed to forget about geometry and reach out, billow, and rumple for a less studied, more casual effect. The result isn't the strictly controlled environment defined by a perfectly clipped hedge, but it is just as efficient at giving privacy and shelter.

Shrub border. Remember the shrubberies into which heroines of Victorian novels were always fleeing for a good weep? A procession of various deciduous shrubs and evergreens still works as a romantic backdrop for garden drama, even if the drama is only horticultural. Deployed as a screen behind flower borders, or as an edge to a path or outdoor room, the shrub border relies on contrasts in habit, foliage, texture, flowers, and berries to create a garden where the plants *are* the structure.

Hedgerow. A standard feature of the agricultural landscape in Europe and much of North America, hedgerows are hodgepodge hedges—a mix of trees, a bunch of trees and shrubs, even brambles—that serve as a windbreak, a boundary between fields, or a barrier to keep animals from wandering. Hedgerows need ample acreage in which to unfold as a feature of an artfully rural garden, suggesting far-off fields, meadows, and scenic surprises, even when there aren't any.

CHANGES IN ELEVATION

By molding a hillside into stepped terraces *(left)*, retaining walls make room for dense, complex plantings in the beautifully compact garden of Sherna and Kipp Stewart, at Big Sur, California. Acanthus, santolina, and ceanothus soften the stonework. Wide, solid stairs, carved out of the slope, invite you to climb from a sunny gravel-covered terrace onto higher ground, and the cool shade of a wooden pergola.

ROOM WITHOUT WALLS

Just as a blanket puts dibs on your spot at the beach, a brick carpet, designed by Margaret Kerr *(right)*, stakes out a living area in the garden. (This may look like a throw rug, but it's permanently set in sand, atop a sturdy landscape-fabric liner held in place by a steel frame.) The minimalist bench indicates that this is also an area for quiet contemplation, whether you scrutinize the figured brick tapestry or turn to gaze at the wilder patterns of the woods.

boundaries

ESPALIER AS WALL RELIEF

In Europe, centuries ago, *espalier* meant the wooden frame onto which the branches of a tree or shrub were tied, trained, and pruned to grow flat; today, the word refers to the plant or the training technique itself. The desired posture a maturing espalier takes on can be informal or geometric, like this candelabra-form pear tree *(left)* that John Saladino underplanted with baby's breath. Espaliers also provide an efficient way to fit various kinds of trees into small spaces, either grown against solid walls, as here, or along freestanding trellises or fences.

WALL AS PLANT GALLERY

This 20-foot-high stuccoed wall *(right)* might induce claustrophobia if it were left unadorned. Instead, the resourceful owner, Ted Newbold, in Philadelphia, Pennsylvania, conceived the idea of garden as gallery. After painting the surface a pale neutral, he mounted his collection of salvaged cornices, capitals, and other architectural artifacts, some of which support planters.

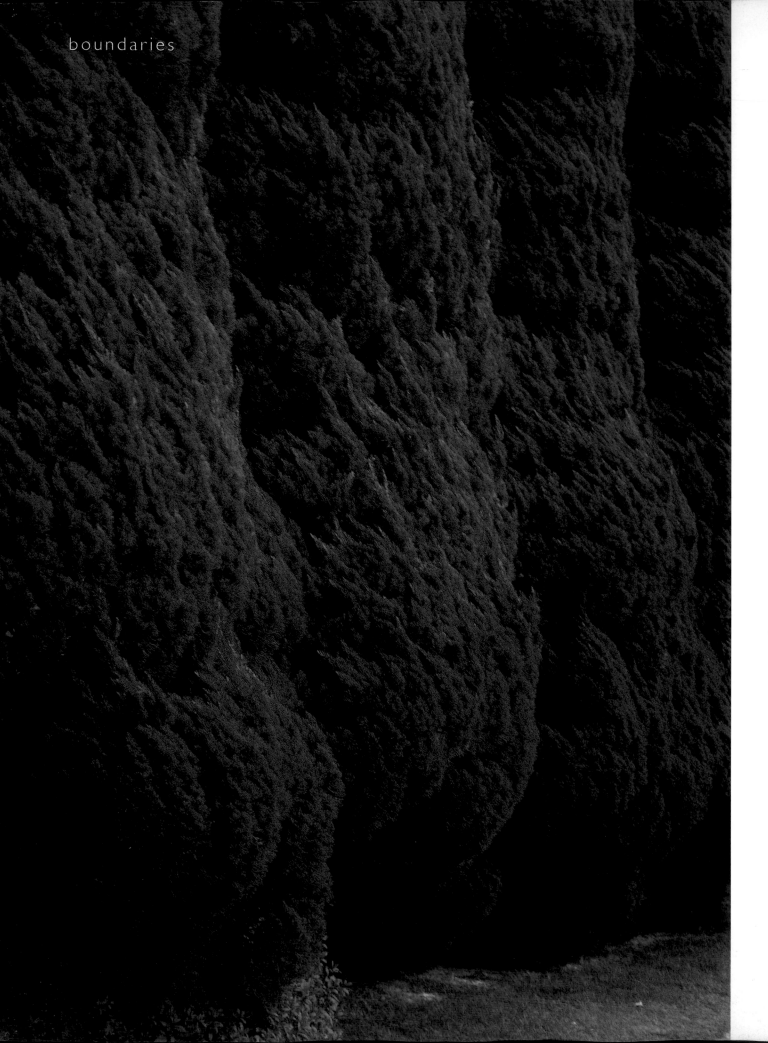

FLOWING HEDGE

Even without a hint of a breeze, you would swear that this row of junipers, *Juniperus chinensis* 'Kaizuka', billows, ebbs, and flows *(left)*. The effect is as soothing as rippling water, and yet, as the trees grow up and out, they supply a stout windbreak and reliable all-season definition in the landscape. Their fluid contours result from the juniper's natural growth habit; not a twig has ever been touched by shears or clippers.

TUMBLING WALL

Like some glacial riverbed heaved out of primordial hills, this wall *(right)* appears to have emerged from its terrain, solid and immutable. The stones were indeed unearthed from the parched land of Sonoma, California, where designers Louise La Palme Mann and Ron Mann have made their home. But every last rock has been placed meticulously by mason Jeronimo Pérez. Rather than turning the wall into a cozy rockery, with plants spilling out of every crevice, it has been left austere. If the masonry looks natural, the orbs on top of it (crafted from wine-barrel hoops) assert that there's a human force at work.

boundaries

WALLS

Geometric masonry. This is the wall to bound a garden laid out in geometric beds. Stucco, adobe, brick, or ashlar (square-hewn) stone all lend themselves to precise formality; the higher the wall, the thicker it needs to be for stability. If you opt for brick, the more complex the bond (the pattern in which bricks are laid), the richer the texture. Whether a wall is two feet high or ten, top it with an elegant stone cap or brick coping.

Rustic masonry. Rough-hewn rock, pieced together with or without mortar, lacks the conspicuous regularity of ashlar masonry or brickwork, even though its homespun look may demand just as much concentration—and more ingenuity—to assemble. This is the wall to border a rambling woodland garden, a meadow, or a hidden pond. If you don't lay the stones with mortar, shove soil into the crevices and plant them with sedum, *Alyssum montanum*, *Aurinia saxatilis*, or *Cerastium tomentosum*.

Trellis and lattice. A network of intersecting lengths of milled lumber or natural branches, a trellis gives climbing plants a structure to grip; the finer crisscross of woven or overlapping laths that makes up latticework also filters light and lets breezes in. These structures may look like filigree, but they must be strong enough to withstand weather and aggressive plants.

Retaining wall. Like the buttress holding up a cathedral, a retaining wall holds up the earth. It can support a garden terrace carved from an existing hillside, or it can be built beside a slope, and then filled with soil to create a new level of flat land. A garden staircase is really a series of tiny retaining walls.

Ha-ha. Where you need a solid barrier, but don't want to block the view, what do you do? Scoop a deep trench between the garden and the outlying land, and install a sunken wall that surprises unsuspecting visitors who step to the brink. Ha-ha! The laugh's also on ravenous herbivores like deer, who can't get in.

PLANTS EDGED IN STONE

Even one carefully chiseled piece of architecture, such as this formal limestone parapet by Texas garden designer James David *(left)*, imparts a reassuring sense of certainty. "This is where everything's meant to be," such walls seem to say. "This is the gardener's hand and vision at work." Having been assigned their places, the plants do the rest, though not entirely as they please. The boxwood and a cone of dwarf yaupon, a holly native to the South, are neatly clipped. A rough granite sphere found in a nearby riverbed adds to this garden's robust geometry.

PLANTS EDGED IN PLANTS

Any gardener could do what Bennett Baxley has done on his South Carolina farm *(right)* even with different kinds of trees, potted plants, and shrubs making up the hedge that's squared around them. Here, the hedge is clipped abelia, the trees are crape myrtle, and the potted plants (which Baxley rotates throughout the season) include tall blue agapanthus, underplanted with purple petunias. The hedge provides continuous structure while the crape myrtles supply asymmetry to temper the formality.

boundaries

STRADDLING THE FENCE

Back when rodeos and square dances were the only events where dungarees qualified as adult dress-up attire, split-rail fences were strictly for farm fields, paddocks, and the outer limits of suburban lawns. Blue jeans go nearly everywhere now, and the rustic-only fence of yesteryear is right at home in glamorous company. The owners of this Long Island garden originally put up a split-rail fence to line a simple vegetable patch. Later, they replaced the humble beds of edibles with grand perennial borders, but never got around to "upgrading" the fence. As it turns out, this delay was all to the good: the weathered timbers help to leaven the grandeur of the borders and their honor guard of upright evergreens.

F E N C E S

Split-rail. Although there are many variations on this all-American rustic theme (Virginia's so-called worm fence zigzags, for example, while Wyoming's buck fence crisscrosses), split-rail fences invariably consist of rough-hewn rails wedged into or thrust between upright posts. The rugged texture of the wood is a pleasing reminder of the simple tools and the patient craft that go into their construction.

Picket. Our collective memory takes picket fences back only to Colonial America, but in fact they were prominent features in Chinese pleasure grounds 1,200 years ago, and bounded many a medieval garden. Unadorned or embellished with cutouts, painted or bare, they still convey a sense of well-ordered domesticity. And because gaps between the pickets allow glimpses of the property within, such fences also signal a genuine, if discreet, welcome.

Close-board. "Beyond the pale" now means out of line, but during the Middle Ages it meant outside the row of pales (and posts) that composed a proper close-board fence, uptight cousin of the picket. From a prefab stockade to a more stately wall of planks and finials, a close-board fence quickly frames a private outdoor room—and an instant backdrop for a newly planted border.

Wattle. Picture a garden in a basket, and the allure of wattle (woven wood or wicker) fences becomes clear. Interlacing willow wands can be almost formal, like a game of cat's cradle stretched across the land. Twisted native cedar branches, with the bark left on, are as genteelly rustic as an Adirondack-twig porch rocker.

Metal. Whether it is wrought or cast, a fine iron fence asks to be admired as a work of art; you'd think twice before letting morning glories smother it. Ornate forged screens and railings were first used to enclose cathedral sanctuaries, and even today a metal gate or grille promises someplace special on the other side.

structures

STRIP AWAY ALL the plants from a garden, and what do you have? The structure (and the structures) that reminds you that here is space organized by human hands, for human needs as well as nature's. Many of us take to gardening because we think it might be fun to grow things, realizing later, sometimes much later, as our design sense matures, that we want to do a better job of framing, encasing, setting off the plants—and the spaces they inhabit. It's not just plants that bring a style to a garden; it's the structural choices you make that give it character, whimsy, grandeur, intimacy, serenity: flair. The structural elements you include are every bit as important as the natural elements; walk through a garden, for example, and you'll find your eye drawn as much to things that are fixed in place as it is to living things, which move, sway, and change shape through the seasons. Structures ground the garden and, because they're fixed, they enable you to watch the garden grow, just as notches in a doorjamb can chart a child's progress. And in the end, plants that climb will do much better with something to climb on, and plants that spill over will need something to spill over. Structures make the garden possible.

There are two kinds of garden rooms. The first is horticultural, walled off somehow, its structure determined by the nature of the plantings. The second is a literal structure, offering shelter and shade, a place to view the garden and live in it yet slightly apart. It may be open to the elements—a gazebo, a pergola, even a screened porch. Or it may be closed off, like a shed, a glass-walled greenhouse, even a child's playhouse. In any case, it's integral to the design and to the way the garden is to be used.

In choosing your fixed elements—everything from obelisks to arbors to ornaments— you're expressing your personal taste. A Roman cherub conveys a classical mood, a stone Japanese lantern a far sparer one. (For that matter, pink flamingos and cutout tires send messages as well, but quite different ones.) A freestanding arbor invites you to walk through it; a pergola invites you to stop. Patterns and textures you build onto walls or lay into the soil make ornate statements and add to the intricacy of design. Set out some plants in pots, and you're highlighting them visually; pots are structural. Ultimately, what you bring to the garden is what you bring into it.

RUSTIC ARBOR

Cedar trunks with the bark left on frame interior designer John Saladino's stylishly countrified arbor, near the outstretched wings of a topiary bird. Over time, the timber structure will be veiled in clematis and silverlace vine. Flagstones pave the arbor floor, subtly echoing the solid geometry of a wall banked with peonies and iris.

GRACIOUS GAZEBO
This neo-Georgian brick gazebo *(left)*, at the Winterthur Museum and Garden in Delaware, was designed as a sheltered viewing stand from which to admire tableaux of spring blooms. *Viburnum macrocephalum* and *V. plicatum tomentosum* are in flower beside the lawn; mowers have skirted clusters of post-bloom daffodil foliage, leaving cloud-like patterns on the green.

LEAFY ALCOVE
Six *Hydrangea paniculata* 'Grandiflora'—trained into standards and underplanted with Korean box—create an airy poolside breakfast nook *(right)* at the Long Island retreat of Larry and Jody Carlson. The only solid structure in this corner of the L-shaped "room" is brick paving.

SCREEN PORCH

Reminiscent of those little mesh domes you put over a cake to keep the bugs away, this screen porch *(left)* designed by Lester Collins is about as diaphanous as an outdoor room can be. Here, you're overlooking the lake at Innisfree, the public garden near Millbrook, New York. But the simple design, scaled bigger or smaller (this one is 16 by 26 feet), would work anywhere you had a view, and wanted an outdoor room from which to view it. Use weatherproof pressure-treated wood for the frame, concrete bricks for the pilings, and wire screening for the open panels, covering the unsightly staples (which attach screening to wood) with moldings for a finished look. Make the ceiling detachable (with metal hooks), for winter storage, and tilt the floor imperceptibly, for rain runoff, covering drainage holes with screening.

SUN-DAPPLED DECK

The post-and-beam redwood structure of Sherna and Kipp Stewart's California pergola *(right)* is simplicity itself. Decorative patterns come from shadows cast by the roof trellis and from the textures and colors of plants: datura and agapanthus at eye level, Burmese honeysuckle trailing overhead.

Arbor. The basic definition of this widely—and loosely—applied term is "a freestanding structure, with an openwork roof, on which to grow plants." From there, the possible variations—impeccably classical or quirkily picturesque; supported by white-painted columns or by bark-clad tree trunks; coiled by one svelte vine or lost in a tangle of climbers—are endless. An arbor is an architectural hybrid: a peekaboo retreat but not a shelter; part building, part vegetation, the centaur of the garden. The dimensions of an arbor must be determined by the size and strength of its twining companion (wisteria, for instance, is a no-holds-barred wrestler; morning glory, a lightweight) as well as the scale of the landscape. In general, the huskier the better, to avoid the look of a matchstick hut awaiting the Big Bad Wolf.

Pergola. The word comes from the Latin *pergula,* meaning "projection," and indeed, a pergola often is a garden structure that projects from a wall of another building, so that one of its sides is solid; the rest of the structure is posts or columns, with open beams lying flat across the top, to bear the climbing plants that will eventually turn it into a shelter (it's the lack of a sloping, continuous roof that distinguishes it from a porch). Many a pergola, however, stands free of other buildings—so how does it differ from an arbor? Well, nobody ever claimed that garden nomenclature is infallibly precise. A pergola *is* a kind of arbor, but one that belongs at the more architectural, classical, geometric, formal, substantial end of the design spectrum. It's your call.

Arch. Framing a gate, a view, the start of a path, or a seat for resting along the way, this round-topped portal stands in the garden like a doorway or a window that has broken free of solid walls. Climbing plants root it to the land.

Gallery. Also known as a tunnel. *Another* arbor variant: a linked series of metal or lath arches so slender that they tend to vanish amid twining vines or supple trees (laburnum is a favorite).

GARDEN GOD

Regardless of how obsessed with plants we become, our attention is still instinctively drawn to our own species in the landscape—animate or not. The eye-catching human figure at the end of this gravel-paved path *(opposite)* is a statue of Mercury. The parterre over which he presides was created at London's Chelsea Flower Show by Clifton Landscape and Design. Clipped cones of boxwood and triangular beds of lavender, sage, and allium all point toward the garden's resident deity.

Statuary. If you install a statue in the garden—a carved wooden squirrel atop a gatepost; a marble nymph on a pedestal; a terra-cotta mask hung on a wall; a contemporary abstract metal stabile on the lawn; even a pink plastic flamingo by the front walk—you're doing what gardeners have always done: populating the landscape with an embodiment of your own taste and fantasies, emphasizing a key point in your design, and offering up art to the elements. As statues acquire a patina of verdigris or rust, lichen or moss, and their edges are worn by wind and rain, they bear witness to inevitable growth and change.

Obelisk. A four-sided tapered monolithic shaft with a pyramid at the tip, the obelisk was erected by Egyptians as a tribute to the sun god. It remains an iconic shape (think of the Washington Monument). Georgian country squires used obelisks to endow new pleasure grounds with the gravitas of antiquity. Today, an obelisk punctuates the land like an exclamation point.

Urn. For a plantable container to qualify for urn status, it should come with its own base (or pedestal, for real grandeur), and must have a shapely profile, with or without handles. Paired with a twin on either side of a doorway, gate, or stairway, or evenly lined up with several mates at the edge of a terrace, an urn is the basic ingredient for foolproof formality. On its own, a handsome urn is an effective centerpiece in a garden bed.

Sundial. The upright gnomon of a sundial tells the time of day by casting a shadow across the plane on which it's mounted, either horizontally, on a pedestal, or vertically, against a wall. It need not be antique or inscribed *Tempus fugit* to symbolize history and remind you of the quick passage of time on a summer's day.

Birdbath. At first glance, it's merely a basin on a pedestal. But a birdbath is also a structural element, for gardens of any size, that comes to life with the chatter, flutter, and splash of wildlife on the wing.

structures

R O O M S

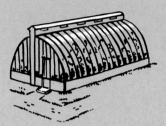

Greenhouse. The greenhouse (or glasshouse) is a potting shed
with walls and a roof of glass panels set in wooden or metal frames. It is
both a horticultural workshop and an adaptable microclimate for growing
seedlings, protecting tender plants, propagating, and puttering.

Conservatory. With the surge in exotic flora arriving in Europe
and America late in the eighteenth century, conservatories—ornamental
glasshouses cum sitting rooms—became fashionable additions to the
homes of the well-to-do. Today, with more efficient building materials
(such as insulated glass), climate control, and prefab parts, they're more
accessible than ever before, and more practical as all-season living rooms.

Terrace. By any other name (such as patio or deck) a platform
without walls or roof may be furnished, and used, like many of the
rooms *inside* a house. A terrace may provide an alcove for dining, a space
for cooking, a chaise for napping, an umbrella or a tree for a private
canopy of shade. Brick, flagstone, planks, and gravel are common paving
materials; it's safest to choose colors and textures that reflect those of
house and garden.

Porch. This is the quintessential indoor/outdoor room, a roofed
terrace that projects from the house. A screen porch, enclosed by panels
of fine wire or plastic mesh, admits views and breezes while excluding
pests. The equivalent of a sweater draped around your shoulders, in case
you might need it, a porch enables you to luxuriate in nature without
feeling exposed.

Gazebo. The grown-up version of a playhouse is a gazebo, a freestanding roofed pavilion with no express purpose except as a sheltered
spot for sipping tea or cocktails, drinking in the fine points of a landscape,
or musing over etymology (does "gazebo" really derive from the Latin
videbo, "I shall see," or is it an English corruption of the French *Ça c'est beau,*
"That's beautiful"?).

PARTY PERGOLA

Within the framework of a garden room—arbor, pergola, or porch—a picnic is an all-out occasion. There is no ironclad rule stating that alfresco meals must be a matter of paper plates, plastic forks, and citronella bug lights. This classical pergola *(left)* has been dressed for the evening with "indoor" finery: hemstitched linens, crystal stemware, china, and brass candelabras. Garden designer Jon Carloftis planted the backdrop of paper birch, American boxwood, cypress, artemisia, and English ivy.

SHY STATUE

Tucked-away ornaments give a garden the aura of a richly layered past, besides implying that the more you explore the more you'll discover. You might miss this chipped bust *(right)* nestled amid the ivy on the first pass, but you'd catch it, surely, on the second.

LIVABLE CONSERVATORY

Constructing a conservatory for year-round living is not a do-it-yourself project. To begin with, like any dwelling, it needs a foundation, which requires excavating below the frost line, setting footings, and pouring concrete. The Long Island conservatory on these pages combines custom design with stock builder's parts: off-the-shelf double-hung windows, French doors, and aluminum framing bars, plus lumber-yard red cedar. Tempered glass panels from an industrial supplier are sealed to the frame with commercial silicon glazing compound. In summer, owners Joe Petrocik and Myron Clement use the ceiling fan to draw breezes in from the garden. In winter, electric baseboard heating keeps the interior snug.

pathways

IS THERE ANYTHING more seductive than a garden gate ajar, with a path inside it, leading—who knows where? Wouldn't you do just about anything to find out?

That's what pathways can do, draw you in, compel you through a garden, let it reveal itself slowly, show you surprises along the way, save the best for last, or wind around and have you end up somewhere else. Paths can create new spaces for plants, and make it easier to get to those plants by providing a clear surface that makes it possible to maneuver a lawn mower or wheelbarrow. Even the suggestion of a pathway (flagstones, say, laid a foot apart through a lawn leading toward whatever comes next) implies destination. Better yet are steps, creating mystery by changing the levels of the land, and creating a profound sense of drama—there's nothing like the sound of shoes moving up or down on stone steps. Paths and steps—a garden's story is always told in its progression.

Whereas the touch required with plants is tender but firm, carving out pathways demands boldness. First, you envision the space, then you conquer it by dividing it. You're not adding something to the land, you're actually changing the landscape by using serious materials, and that demands a commitment.

In designing and planting a garden one room at a time, the way most of us do it, pathways are the links that signal transition, telling you where to stop, and where to start up again. The more varied you can make them—wood chips on a woodland area, gravel paths in an herb garden, bricks patterned on an outdoor dining room—the richer the tapestry on the garden floor, the more complex the garden.

And don't forget to carpet the staircases.

One of the great concessions I made when we bought our house was to give up slopes; I love slopes, the idea of steps and levels and terraces, but our land is as flat as a failed soufflé. Except in one place. The terrace leads both straight back from the house and toward a very small square of grass at the side, which I'm slowly planting with shrubs and a few flowers. From terrace to grass is, if you really stretch your imagination, a slope, barely discernible. "I see a step here," a gardening friend of mine said when he first saw the property. "We can just carve out a step." It's a stretch of the imagination, but it's also a step carved in stone.

RAMBLING BOARDWALK
How do you get from the shady grove in which you stand to the lake that glimmers beyond that sunny patch of lawn? A meandering path of shredded bark or pine needles might have done the trick, but would blend into the landscape, not define it. Here, at Innisfree, near Millbrook, New York, the walkway is elevated into a magical footbridge on dry land, which zigzags among the ferns. Like much of Innisfree, which is open to the public, the boardwalk was inspired by Asian gardens, where the experience of treading a beautiful bridge or path is a pleasure to be savored as an end in itself.

STAIRS WITH A POINT

Like unexpected crosscurrents that jolt you in a canoe, these angled bluestone steps *(left)* call you to attention on a garden walk. Suddenly, the automatic, everyday activity of climbing up or down becomes an adventure. And as you navigate the steps you can ponder the marvel of solid slabs that appear to hover like the cantilevered balconies of Frank Lloyd Wright's masterpiece, the house called Fallingwater.

A THRESHOLD TO CROSS

There are houses where you have to search for some sign of a path into the garden. Not in the garden of Robert Jakob and David White *(right)*. There's no deck, patio, porch, or terrace separating house from garden. Framed by French doors, the straight bluestone path unfurls like a carpet rolled out for royalty, just a step away from the plank floor inside.

ROUNDABOUT ROUTE

It's usually sensible to plot a garden path as the shortest distance between two points, but there's room for a planned diversion now and then. No one would quibble over the extra minutes it takes to walk around the splendid urn that links the otherwise straight bluestone path down the middle of Joanna Reed's Pennsylvania parterre. Like any genuine centerpiece, the urn seems to proclaim: "Whatever else you have on your mind, wherever else you *think* you're going, stop for a moment and look where you are. You have arrived."

Straight path. If a garden were a mystery novel, its path would be its plot, and a straight path is one of those tales that discloses the ending right at the start. The enjoyment lies in the ingenious revelation of details that lead to the inevitable climax. When a straight path—of gravel, brick, or symmetrically laid flagstones—bisects a garden, it usually implies geometric formality in the overall landscape design. Make a path broad enough for two people to walk abreast, and it will seem hospitable; any narrower than that, and it becomes a place for solitary pursuits.

Allée. The Persians were the first to turn a straight path into an avenue—*allée* in French—by planting parallel rows of evenly spaced trees. During the Renaissance, this formation was used to frame a dramatic approach to a building or to create stately horticultural corridors among garden rooms. As an organizing principle, it is as valid today as it was then. An allée of shade trees may take decades to mature, but faster, smaller-scale results can be accomplished with shrubs or other plants in large pots.

Winding path. Here, the plot of a garden reveals its mysteries slowly, and it only becomes clear that the end is in sight when it truly is. Although serpentine paths were long a feature of Chinese gardens, they didn't turn up as a fashion in the West until the first half of the eighteenth century, when English landscapers began to loosen up the geometry that had reigned in European gardens since the Middle Ages. Even when a garden is intricately contrived, meandering paths feel relaxed and spontaneous.

Stepping stones. Flat stones spaced a step or so apart present a connect-the-dots game, either on dry land or crossing a stream. Tucked into a wide border, stepping stones are unobtrusive places to stand or crouch for deadheading and weeding without crushing plants underfoot.

Bridge. Whether it's a stone arch or a log, a bridge does more than cross water. A bridge in the style of the house unites a formal landscape; a bridge of rugged timber eases the transition from garden to wilderness.

JUNGLE TRAIL

Were it not for the scored-concrete path to the front door of Suzanne Lipschutz's Miami house *(left),* a visitor might hesitate to venture into the jungle that seems ready to gobble up the yard. But the smooth surface of the pavers and the skill with which they have been fitted together like a puzzle—as well as the reassuring glimpse of lantern and gate at the end of the path—signal that civilization holds the upper hand. *Rhoeo spathacea* creeps along the path. *Datura metel* 'Flore Pleno' peeks out from the right, and *Pennisetum* 'Burgundy Giant' shoots up at left. Near the red door, royal and traveler palms add height, while allamanda climbs above.

STEPS AS SCULPTURE

Designed by Maryland landscape architect Priscilla Botacchi, exquisite quarried-stone stairs *(right)* are recessed into subtle terracing. Because the risers extend beyond the ends of the inset treads, the entire staircase poses a delightful enigma: is the turf encroaching on the steps, or are buried steps emerging from the ground? Coupled with the rhythmic play of light and shadow, this mystery makes the stairs an arresting piece of minimalist sculpture.

pathways

STREAM OF STEPS

A stairway of gently rounded stones
(left) runs through Timothy Maxson's
Northern California garden like a dry
streambed, linking a small studio at
the crest of the hillside property
with the main house 50 feet below.
Maxson had a local farmer bulldoze the
path of the stairs from the soil before
he set genuine river stones in mortar.
He then bordered the steps with
oregano, *Plectostachys serphyllifolia*,
lavender, and silvery olive trees.

DUGOUT STEPS

On steeply sloping ground where
the look is rustic and no exposed tree
roots offer a foothold, rudimentary
stairs of soil packed behind planks
make sense. Mix the dirt with gravel,
for good drainage; don't put peat moss
into the mix, or you'll be walking on a
sponge. South Pasadena designers
Stamps & Stamps devised these
earthen steps *(right)* in collaboration
with landscape gardener Jack Uribe,
an expert on desert plants that
suited the site, one-third of an acre
in Los Angeles. Flanking the hillclimb
are *Senecio mandraliscae (near right)*
and spiky century plant *(far right)*.

FILLING THE CRACKS

Gardeners have always planted
between the stones of paths and
terraces—to soften a dull expanse
of masonry with green and to
emphasize the pattern of the paving.
Landscape architect Pamela Burton
has accomplished both goals in this
courtyard *(left)*, though on a giant
scale that heightens the impact of
plain geometry. Burton has seeded
grass between these pavers, but in
similar spots with plenty of sun,
herbs like creeping thyme would
be aromatic alternatives.

VANISHING STONES

The proportion of solid paving to
green matter in Pamela Burton's
courtyard is reversed in the backyard
of landscape designer Kirsten Berg
(right), where stepping stones almost
sink into the sea of lawn. Western
maidenhair fern, *Adiantum aleuticum*,
heads the perennial border *(near right)*
that parallels the vegetable patch *(far
right)*. The shed is draped in flowering
potato vine, *Solanum jasminoides*.

pathways

STEPS FOR DISPLAY

A slight change of level, with a short flight of connecting steps, can play an ornamental role that far outweighs its utilitarian function. This stone staircase, between a sunken entryway and a higher terrace, acts as a multilevel stage for a movable show of potted plants starring white lilies, Canterbury bells, santolina, ivy, and petunias.

Formal stairs. A formal stairway doesn't have to look as if it were designed for crinolined ladies to descend. Like "formal" design any-where in a landscape, it is unmistakably a human artifact, a deliberate work of reason and skill, not a random act of nature—it has been *formed* as part of an orderly, usually symmetrical, pattern. The geometry of formal stairs may rely on straight lines or curves, or on a harmonious combination of both; their grace depends on a comfortable ratio of tread to riser: both the climb and the descent should feel perfectly choreographed—a pleasure, not an effort. Constructed of brick, stone, or wood, such stairs glorify the everyday ceremonies of life in the garden.

Informal steps. This is architecture that's meant to appear as if hardly any of it has actually been constructed; it achieves its purpose if it virtually *dis*appears into the woods, a rocky hillside, a meadow bank, or other natural landscape. Any of a variety of available materials will do the trick—split or unsplit logs, fieldstone, rough-hewn planks, even tree stumps or packed soil—whatever helps your feet manage the slope with-out distracting your eyes from the scenery. The desired effect is enhanced by plants growing up, down, and over the edges of the steps.

Terrace. It's easy enough to see a hillside terrace as one step of a giant stairway that levels sloping ground. A terrace can also be a deck or patio that provides a livable solid, flat surface without any earth-moving. Either way, constructing a terrace is never simple, but the rewards are both utilitarian and aesthetic: leveling part of a hillside promotes water reten-tion, reduces erosion, and eases the gardener's tasks, but it also makes for wonderful views and a fine array of railings, balustrades, and human-scale stairs. The raised edge of a terrace is an ideal place to sit, to grow trailing plants, or to mount a statue where it can stand against the sky.

Ramp. A stairway without steps, a path that tilts up off the ground—a ramp ensures a firm footing in uneven terrain and safe passage for wheel-chairs, strollers, tricycles, and wheelbarrows.

DISAPPEARING PAVERS

Viewed from the side, this grid of neat white squares *(left)* almost vanishes into the lawn. Flush with the ground and barely a few inches square, they are the projecting tops of much larger waffle-iron-shaped concrete slabs whose soil-filled grooves are seeded with grass. Known as grass blocks, the pavers were invented in Europe as a discreet remedy for vanishing green space and wasteful storm-water runoff; for good drainage, the perforated slabs are laid on a bed of sand. They are now manufactured in the United States (available through masonry suppliers), where they are used for everything from driveways to golf-cart trails. Grass shaded by a vehicle longer than a day or so is likely to yellow, and because the slab conducts heat, frequent watering is a must during dry spells. Mix Kentucky bluegrass with other more heat-tolerant fescues.

STAIRWAY TO EXPLORE

Native-plant specialist Roger Raiche used discarded highway concrete to build a ruggedly exotic stairway *(right)* in the quarter-acre he shares with garden designer Tom Chakas, in Berkeley, California. Like a treasure hunt through the ruins of a lost civilization, a trek up the steps leads past an intriguing mix of hand-picked rubble, sculptural salvage, and stunning plants: yellow-flowering *Homeria ochroleuca* and *Kniphofia uvaria,* gray-leaved *Verbascum bombyciferum,* and a columnar cactus, *Echinopsis pachanoi.*

PATH AS GARDEN

Unused until late June, when it becomes the major path to a swimming pool, this quarried limestone walk in Chicago *(left)* was a springtime eyesore until James Grigsby, of Craig Bergmann Landscape Design, planted it with early bloomers. The floral spectacle, which is timed to end in early June, includes species crocus, *Anemone pulsatilla*, brunnera, creeping phlox, *Iris pumila, I. germanica*, helianthemum, creeping veronica, cranesbill, nepeta, and woolly thyme.

PATH AS FOCAL POINT

Rather than show the way to a distant destination, this path *(right)* leads the eye around and around. Garden designer Lisa Stamm and architect Dale Booher spun this pattern to encircle an upright, grooved millstone outside their house on Shelter Island, New York. Arranged like radiating spokes, the narrow flagstones suggest the rotation of a mill—or the cycle of the seasons. Here, in summer, purple sage rings the central monolith, below a canopy of 'New Dawn' roses.

pathways

COUNTRY BOARDWALK

Constructed of close-spaced pine planks notched into sturdy posts, a boardwalk makes its way around the pond in a Virginia garden *(left)* designed by landscape architects Oehme, van Sweden & Associates of Washington, D.C. The walkway makes the marshy ground accessible for nature walks, for fishing parties, and for excursions by a family member who uses a wheelchair.

MOWN PATH

A few passes of the lawn mower through tall grasses, and you've got yourself a pathway, a riveting axial vista, and an instant frame to define the "wild" garden—native plants, swaying grasses, meadow flowers—on either side *(right)*. All without laying a single paver.

water

reflecting poolswaterfallsstreamsswimming poolsfishpondswater liliesbridgesrecirculating pumpsfountainsmoss

EARTH, AIR, THE FIRE of the sun—and water, the garden's grace note. What is it about water in a garden? Cooling, refreshing, silent, and still, or bubbling, flowing, trickling, it splinters the sun, and deepens with the day; if the rest of the garden tells a story, water keeps its secrets. Maybe it's because water is so essential to replenishing the body and to nature that there isn't a gardener who gardens for long without yearning for a water display. And there isn't a gardener who can't have one. Even a scalloped shell of cement edged in moss or a simple basin filled to the brim will capture the eye, stop it, and soothe it.

When I got married, a close friend asked me what I really wanted for a wedding present, and I told her without hesitating: "a horse trough." She refused, and instead gave me over-size Limoges coffee cups, saucers, and plates, perfect for Sunday morning strawberries and croissants. They're fine, and we use them ritualistically every Sunday, but I would definitely have preferred the horse trough, with which I could have created water in my garden in any of a number of different ways. (You can do wonders with horse troughs.) I'd still love one, and would make good use of it (as would my dogs), but my water dreams are different now. For the scale of my garden and the size of our brick terrace I'd now like a small raised brick pool, with walls that looked like a formal brick wall does, and with water circulating in it, though not bubbling like a fountain. Fish? Maybe. Water lilies? Optional. I want it to be a structural thing, providing the emotional element of water. Any horse troughs that turned up, I'd put somewhere else.

Your choices? There are many, from black fiberglass "ponds" you dig a vast space in the earth for—and they can be lovely—to tiny birdbaths, which, carefully tended, attract birds that bathe—and splatter and shout and preen. As someone prone to entrepreneurial fantasies, I sometimes imagine creating a beautiful terra-cotta pot that's also a fountain. Fill it with water, plug it in, and insert it among other pots on your terrace, where it will bubble a bit—instant fountain. I bet it would sell millions.

REFLECTING POOL
This channel garden, a self-contained room within a larger garden, isn't for swimming, fishing, or strolling reedy banks. Inspired by the owner's love of the formal gardens that surround Italian villas, the barely 16-inch-deep pool is a place for reflection, in both senses of the word—a place for mirroring sky, statue, and trees, as well as for contemplating the serenely composed landscape. Brick edging underscores the geometric relationship between lawn and pool, which in turn align with the house to provide an axial view from the master bedroom.

water

POND IN A MEADOW

In this meadow on the Vermont property of Anne Woodhull and Gordon Thorne *(left)* the soil bulldozed for the pond has a natural clay content that's high enough to retard seepage on its own. Water is replenished by a spring. Without any further encouragement, ducks and muskrats have settled in among the ornamental grasses and irises that Woodhull and Thorne put into their wetland garden.

POND IN A POT

A 20-inch-wide rustic Chinese urn *(right)* creates a miniature water garden when it's planted with moisture lovers like these: *Iris ensata, Juncus* 'Carmen's Japanese' (variegated cat's tail), and *Thalia dealbata*. A galvanized-metal tub or trough would also work as a container. See page 220 for the basics of water gardening at any scale.

WOODLAND POND

A 2,400-square-foot pond designed by Bruce Kelly and David Varnell *(left)* was dug with a backhoe and lined with durable clay-impregnated cloth and a layer of gravel (to prevent loose particles of clay from clouding the water). Because the pond is barely four feet deep, a circulating pump and a filtration system were installed to keep the water from going stagnant. An elegantly spare footbridge, by David Robinson, combines cedar with wood from sustainably harvested *Tabebuia spp.,* a South American tree.

BACKYARD WATERFALL

Holly and Osamu Shimizu designed their two-foot-high waterfall *(right)* to muffle the noise of passing road traffic and airplanes near Washington, D.C. Because their yard is flat, the couple used gravel, rocks, and soil dug from a 16-by-26-foot pool at the base of the fall, to build up high ground for the artificial stream that meanders about six feet before cascading. They constructed the waterfall from flagstones mortared together and supported by the cinder-block wall of the pool. A $1/2$-horsepower pump, submerged at the far end of the pool, recirculates water through 70 feet of $1\frac{1}{2}$-inch-diameter pipe, up to the head of the stream. A valve enables the Shimizus to adjust the force of the flow—and the volume and quality of its splashing. Variegated ivy trails over the rocks, adding its own highlights to the spectacle.

WATER FEATURES

Formal pool. Like a stylized oasis, the rectangular pool was a focal point in Egyptian gardens in the third millennium B.C. Today, regular geometric shapes are still ideal frames within which to showcase the effects of light on water, as well as the beauty of water plants. Rimmed by a firm band of masonry or tile, a formal pool emanates tranquillity into a courtyard or garden room. It may be a shallow sheet of water, to mirror passing clouds or catch a fountain's runoff, or it may be a tank whose cool depth invites swimmers to take the plunge.

Pond. Either man-made or conveniently provided by nature, a pond takes its contours from the lay of the land around it, giving the appearance that it has always been right where it is. Plant marsh grasses, flag irises, cattails, and other wetlands vegetation to blur the sinuous shoreline, enhancing the effect of a seamless habitat (and masking the lip of a synthetic pond liner). Unlike a formal pool, which demands a position, a pond belongs a little off to the side so that you can rediscover it time and again.

Stream. Call it a creek, brook, arroyo, rill—water that meanders, wriggles, and tumbles like a small river is a dynamic force in the garden. Given an adequate water supply, you can play God by digging a trench, installing a plastic liner and a pump, and gathering rocks to make your own streambed. A garden laid out on geometric lines often calls for a straight-as-an-arrow channel, essentially a formal stream.

Waterfall. A waterfall gives a garden vertical movement, and refracts the light. It can be a liquid sheet constantly flowing over a smooth surface, it can trickle in an uneven stream, or it can plunge in a series of cataracts. The longer the drop, the louder the splash.

Fountain. Whether it's a spouting sculpture, a brimming vessel, or an upturned nozzle that spews its geyser skyward, every fountain is an aria in the garden—a celebration of limitless capabilities.

SWIMMING POOL OASIS

An ordinary swimming pool became an ornamental reflecting pool and a seating area, too, when Pamela Burton rimmed it with a bench-height ledge of Vermont slate. The rose-covered pergola in the background gives the pool a larger architectural frame, while furnishing shade and shelter like the peristyle in a Pompeiian villa.

SWIMMING HOLE

The summertime hangout *(left)* is given shape and structure by the dam that doubles as diving platform, dock, and bench. Set in a meadow of grasses and wildflowers, this is a timeless hideaway where you can imagine dangling your feet and dawdling away an afternoon.

SMALL FISH POND

This man-made backyard pond *(right)* houses koi, which the owners' granddaughters like to feed. Landscape architect Christopher LaGuardia felt that a circle or ellipse would be too formal for the setting, a rustic bayberry grove. He spent a week drawing irregularly curved outlines directly on the soil, using a stick and orange marker paint. After the hole had been dug, a gunite shell, one to three feet deep, was sprayed to line the pond as if it were to be a swimming pool. A layer of gravel was spread to texture the floor, and limestone ledges were installed to give the fish shelter from angling raccoons and cats. (These ledges also conceal ultraviolet-light filters that kill algae, keeping the water crystal clear for viewing the fish.) Glacial boulders were placed here and there with artful "naturalness," as were clumps of abelia, iris, Japanese holly, and mugo pine.

PLANTS AS DESIGN TOOLS

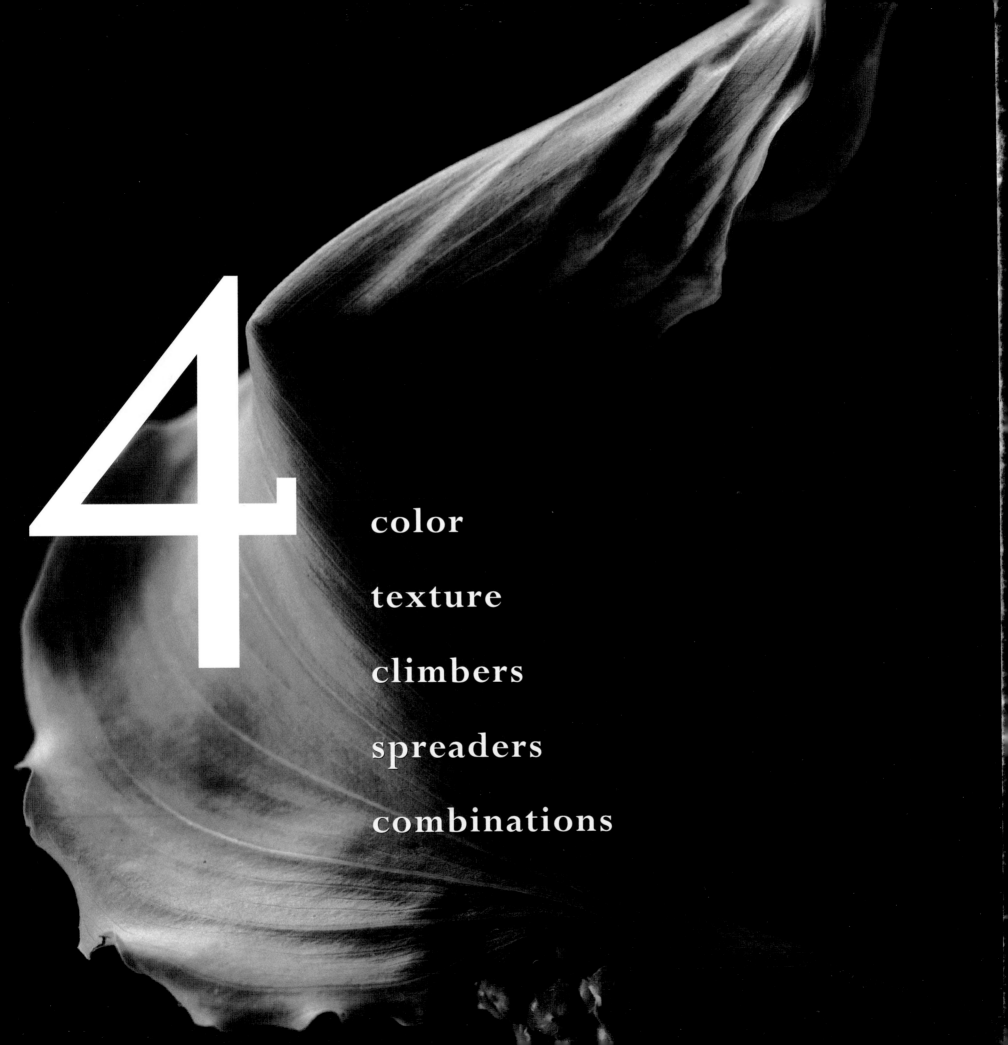

4

color

texture

climbers

spreaders

combinations

THERE ARE MANY GREAT encyclopedic guides out there that will tell you what plants *are*. But in the intimate collaboration between gardener and plants that results in a garden, it's fair for the gardener to ask of plants: What can you *do*? The answers are surprisingly varied. For most of us, the learning curve begins with looking hard at a plant—in a nursery, or in a glossy catalogue photograph—to study it in full bloom. What most of us realize only gradually is just how ephemeral a flower's beauty is. To understand how plants can work, you must put aside the distraction of that fleeting splendor and consider their essential character. In this chapter we have assembled a highly subjective list of hard-working plants with looks *and* personality. The list isn't meant to define a complete horticultural tool chest, but master even a handful of our favorites, and you'll have a versatile kit of parts to build upon.

A really instructive way to study plants as design tools is to visit a great garden many times over the course of a year. As each season progresses, and the plants go in and out of their cycles of bloom, observe the way the garden changes, too. Maybe a corner of a bed that's mostly pastel pink with tulips and peonies in spring, will turn predominantly yellow in midsummer as rudbeckia and coreopsis take over. Certain groupings of plants might attract your attention. But note, too, the way the most striking plants in the garden interact with other, less obvious elements of the landscape. Does it take a backdrop of darker green foliage to set off their color? What other plants anchor the bed with sturdy stems or massive leaves, so that these wisps of color have something to lean on? Do groundcovers spread under the plants like brush strokes, filling in the bare earth? What's happening in the canopy of shrub and tree branches higher up? Scrutinize the countless gradations in the rich spectrum of the color green. Determine a plant's personality: does it dart up perkily like a daisy, for instance—or does it tumble about like a brazen showgirl of a dahlia? Is the weave of textures subtle or bold? Are the unopened buds as alluring as the flowers they hold? And after the blooms are spent, do the seedheads put on the best show?

A gardener is a conductor, and plants are the instruments that make up the orchestra. Proper tending of the plants aside, there's a discipline involved in getting everyone to play well together. You can't have all wind instruments, or the music would be monotonous; you need strings, percussion, and brass to make the whole thing soar and harmonize. This means that if you want a seductive, complex garden, you need a range of plants that variously trail, climb, lose leaves or remain evergreen, stand up to or bend against the elements, show themselves in all seasons, even sometimes, disappear. And gradually, you'll stop listening for that one note, focusing on that one plant, and hold out for the entire symphony.

What had been a gloomy stretch of shingled wall is now a backdrop for the sumptuous contrasts of rich burgundy *Clematis* 'Ernest Markham' and pale roses. Trained up a simple trellis, the two climbers festoon an exterior mirror that doubles the show.

For many gardeners I've talked to, the next step beyond one single plant, or its flowers, is a preoccupation with plants for the front of the border, the mid-border, and the back of the border. I was obsessed with calculating plant heights for years, forever setting plants in front of or behind one another. Eventually, I learned that this three-tiered approach was almost beside the point. That the gardens I really admired were full of the kind of visual surprise no rigid formula could yield. Plants were staggered, purposely set off-kilter to dramatize contrasts in foliage, and the view through it, of still other plants. Instead of straining to build a colorful climb for the eye, three steps up, I learned to love a garden where you don't notice everything at once.

I began to understand, too, that a bed or border doesn't have to end with the tallest plant. If I added a fence post, for instance, and vines to climb it, the garden could spread beyond its finite boundaries. And I got better after a while at letting my plants do what they do best, rather than trying to make them line up row by row, like schoolchildren posing for a class picture with the short kids in front. I made some notable mistakes (hiding some plants, forgetting others), but by giving the plants their say, I'm further along on the learning curve.

All the plants on the following pages make excellent design tools: they grow startlingly up or lavishly over, billow grandly or form tight little balls, provide alluring color or dramatic texture, and they climb or spread or work together. Learning to look out for shape as well as color, foliage as well as flowers, architecture and not just horticulture, will help you study the plants you already have in your garden, and appraise those you're tempted to add. The choices you make for their placement will enhance your design plan. Treated with respect, many plants seem to learn what's expected of them. The adventure, though, lies in discovering how much you learn from what they do in return.

A flamboyant rosette of satiny leaves native to Central America, the bromeliad *Guzmania sanguinea* starts out green then reddens as the plant matures. Garden plants in the tropics and other warm zones—houseplants and greenhouse specimens everywhere else—bromeliads are guaranteed show-stoppers.

COLOR

In 1908, a visitor described Gertrude Jekyll's autumn border at Munstead Wood: "the colouring is gorgeous…the cool coloured ends have a groundwork of quiet, low-toned bluish green, as of yucca and iris; of bright glaucous blue-green as of crambe and elymus…and of grey and silvery

tones in large masses represented by santolina and *Cineraria maritima*, with white and palest pink and pale flowers only." "In my dreams!" I think, as I read this. But remembering certain home truths about color calms me. First, whichever colors compel you, the object is not to "match," but to blend, diffuse, and enrich the color. A blue scheme dulls if it's all, say, forget-me-not blue. Blue needs every shade of blue, and perhaps shiny green foliage, a touch of matte gray, and a hint of yellow—even red. Bright yellow looks brighter against pale yellows, and greens, grays, and whites. Green is great, but is better still with blue-green, gray-green, and white-green, too. If pink's your key color, then cream, apricot, white, and pale gold will help the pink appear pinker. To make a single color statement you need a whole range of plants.

Artemisia species (*page 162*) are grown for their froth of foliage, which is sparkly silver or muted gray. All of these perennial herbs (there are about 200 species in all) play gentle games with the light, mediating between bold-colored plants or bringing out subtle hues, and visually connecting different parts of the garden as it changes, depending on what's in bloom. Some artemisias are feathery, with a mounded habit that is tidily formal, while others have deeply cut foliage and a more casual, sprawling habit. Plant them in well-drained soil, in full sun, in zones 4–9, depending on the species.

Black Hollyhock, *Alcea rosea* 'Nigra' (*left*), blooms in a silky dark spire up to 6 feet tall. A stylish contrast to almost any other flower, it seems to absorb light and, at the same time, make pastels or vivid colors nearby look even brighter by comparison. This plant's impact in a cottage garden is like that of the slim, glamorous stranger who shows up at a party unexpectedly, dressed entirely in black. Technically a biennial, the black hollyhock should be treated as an annual; if you're lucky, it may self-seed and colonize various parts of your garden. It needs moist, well-drained soil, a spot in full sun where there's plenty of air circulation, and secure staking.

Black Mondo Grass, *Ophiopogon planiscapus* 'Nigrescens', is basic black: You can dress it up, or dress it down. Whether used in a cluster of ornamental grasses or in a naturalized setting, it's sturdy and dramatic, with 6-by-12-inch clumps of straplike, blackish green leaves. On the other hand, as a member of the lily family, *Liliaceae*, it has inherited a grace and delicacy that suit a formal setting, where it shows off creamy white flower spikes followed by black berries—the family trademark. An unusual edging plant, it also adds a fillip to more conventional border combinations. Plant in moist, well-drained soil high in organic matter, in light shade (though it will tolerate sun), in zones 7–9.

Candelabra Primrose, *Primula* spp. (*page 165*), are unsurpassed for a blaze of early spring color. These perennials' botanical name comes from the Latin *primus*, "first," and often they bloom, in gemlike colors, even before the daffodils. Where the classic primrose tucks its blossoms close to the

The dark, twisted branches of threadleaf Japanese maple, *Acer palmatum* 'Dissectum', (*left*) intensify the brilliant autumn color for which this tree is prized. *Opposite:* The pale stamen of a black hollyhock, *Alcea rosea* 'Nigra', glows amid dusky petals.

159

leaves, the candelabra's many whorls of flowers rise above the foliage like candles above a candlestick, or like tiny periscopes. They'll colonize quickly in most locations. Plant in consistently moist soil high in organic matter, in partial shade; zones 6–8.

Canna

Canna garden hybrids (*far right*) belong to a vast genus of tropical plants and have lush flamelike flowers and stunning green, bronze, purple, or variegated foliage. Despite their exotic origin they're easy to grow in a border or on their own, in pots. There are dozens to choose from, ranging in height from 4 to 6 feet (although there are dwarf varieties, too). Cannas need well-drained soil high in organic matter, and full sun. In zones 8–10, their rhizomes can be left in the ground over the winter. Farther north, cut back the leaves after the first frost has hit, and store over the winter indoors at 40 degrees.

Dahlia

Dahlia (*page 163*) is the kind of flower that children draw. Showy and bright, dahlia hybrids come in many crayon colors—red, pink, orange, yellow, white, and apricot, among others. Grown from tuberous roots, the stems rise 1 to 5 feet, depending on which of the more than 3,000 available varieties you choose. Flowers begin blooming in midsummer in the south, and in late summer farther north, lasting till frost. Plant in moist, well-drained soil high in organic matter, in full sun. Below zone 8, lift the tuberous roots after the first frost and store at 40 degrees in dry vermiculite. Tubers may be left in the ground in zones 8–10.

Daylily

Daylily, *Hemerocallis*, available in more than 39,000 named cultivars, covers every shade of the spectrum, from white and palest gold to apricot, orange, crimson, and deep purple. One of the easiest perennials to grow, the daylily got its name because each flower lasts just a day, although each scape produces a succession of daily blooms, as many as 50. Given a few years in a sunny location, a single fan of foliage will multiply into a clump of fans, each with a flower scape. To divide daylilies after they bloom, dig the clumps and cut the roots back by one-third and the foliage by one-half. Division should have 3 to 4 fans and replant in compost-enriched soil; zones 3–10.

Delphinium

Delphinium garden hybrids (*right*) produce some of the bluest blues in the perennial border. Hardier than the pure strains, the hybrids are nonetheless rather short-lived, even in the cool, moist climates they prefer. Gardeners who can't resist these aristocrats replace them when necessary, as if they were annuals. The 2-to-5-foot spires bloom in early summer; taller varieties need individual staking. Besides comprising many tones of blue, colors range from violets and mauves to creams, whites, and yellows, with everything in between. They like moist, well-drained, slightly alkaline soil and full sun, in zones 3–9.

Dew Flower

Dew Flower, *Drosanthemum speciosum*, is an impressive low-growing shrub throughout the year, above all in spring and early summer, when abundant, vibrant orange-to-crimson flowers emerge. The 3-inch leaves curve upward, as if asking for admiration. Plant in well-drained soil, in full sun, in zones 9 and 10.

Euphorbia

Euphorbia, or spurge (*opposite*), would, if it were a kid in high school, definitely be cool, daring to be different for a reason. The species are varied within this genus, but some grow proudly in the shape of a very small shrub, front-of-the-border height, reaching up and out a foot or more, with the leaves growing closely together along the stems. Inconspicuous flowers bloom in spring, but are offset by showy bracts, which open up to the light like disks, in colors ranging from lime green to chartreuse, making you imagine you can actually see the rays of light reaching the plant and creating a really unusual self-contained display that keeps drawing the eye. All euphorbias exude a milky sap that could cause a rash if you're not careful, but otherwise the plant is agreeably easy to grow. Plant in well-drained soil, in full sun, and, depending on the species, in zones 3–10.

Euphorbia (*opposite*) demonstrates that green is far more than a background color for flowers from other parts of the spectrum. The lime-green-to-yellow bracts of this euphorbia make an incandescent display above blue-green leaves that line the stems. *Left*: Cooler pastels tint Delphinium 'Pacific Giant', towering above other delphinium cultivars. Bright white and pink bring out the saturated hues of blue and purple, deep tones that tend to recede from view. *Above*: The striped foliage of *Canna* Tropicanna is as fiery as the flower.

Glory Bush, *Tibouchina urvilleana*, a native of

Brazil, will reach 6 feet or more, with spreading branches lightly covered in velvety, ribbed leaves that take on a faint rosy orange hue. The flowers, which appear from late summer into fall, are cups of light-filtering purple with pink filaments. Once hard to find in the U.S., it's increasingly available and well worth the trouble of seeking it out. In northern climates, it is treated as a tender, potted shrub: during the growing season, set the pot out on a terrace or bury the container in the soil, then bring it indoors before the first frost. Grow in moist, acid, well-drained soil, in full sun; hardy in zones 9 and 10.

Hellebore, *Helleborus orientalis*, the perennial

Lenten rose, blooms bright from late winter into early spring. When planted under deciduous shrubs, it offers lush relief from dormant companions' bare branches. The plant, which self-sows reliably, grows 18 to 24 inches and has glossy, leathery evergreen leaves that create a backdrop for the flowers nodding above them. Depending on the species, flowers range from very dark maroon to pink, cream, and marvelous pale green and are often speckled. Plant them in moist, well-drained soil rich in organic matter, in light shade; zones 5–9.

Houttynia, *Houttynia cordata* 'Chameleon',

is a tricolor ground cover, with heart-shaped leaves of green, cream, and red, gently smudged together; the more sun, the more the red tones will predominate as the season progresses. The leaves emit a fragrant tang of citrus; the white flowers are perfectly fine but hardly noticeable against the vivid leaves. It's a rapid spreader, so keep after it with clippers and spade, or use it in a container as an attractive alternative to ivy. Plant in moist soil in full sun to partial shade; zones 6–9.

The annual *Zinnia* 'Candycane', (*above*) stands out in the company of solid colors. *Right:* A welcome mediator, tactful *Artemisia schmidtiana* 'Silver Mound' is equally adept at easing the clash of hot colors and sparking the blend of dark or pastel tones. *Opposite:* Scarlet *Dahlia* 'Shore Acres' exposes its petals gradually, layer by tantalizing layer.

Japanese Jack-in-the-Pulpit,

Arisaema sikokianum, is an intriguing horticultural collector's item whose mysterious beauty thrives in dappled or deeper shade. The silvery green or green three-lobed leaves haven't even emerged fully when the bloom, a dark purple hooded spathe with a chalky white spadix, appears in April, lasting into May. It requires moist soil high in organic matter, semi- to full shade, in zones 5–9.

Lettuce, *Latuca sativa*, is the name of a host of salad

greens—including looseleaf, butterhead, romaine, and crisphead—but they aren't all green. 'Red Sails' lettuce (*page 165*) raises carmine-edged leaves to the sun. Even the greens are a varied feast for the eye: looseleaf is floppy and relaxed, while romaine grows on the straight and narrow; crisphead grows with frilled edges but curls in tight when mature. Butterhead ('Bibb' is the best-known cultivar) unfurls like an old-fashioned cabbage rose. Lined up in rows, they're an elite corps of amazing, edible grace. Grow during spring and then again in fall in moist, well-drained soil—the richer the better—in full sun.

Ligularia, *Ligularia dentata* 'Desdemona', is

spectacular even before it blooms in late summer. Forming a shrublike mound, 3 or 4 feet high, the heart-shaped leaves are dark green fading to silvery green, and when they're ruffled by a breeze, you glimpse their glossy purple undersides. The orange daisylike flowers grow to 5 inches in diameter. Ligularia can be massed or planted alone as an accent, either in a border with other perennials or amid shrubs. Plant in moisture-retentive soil, in semi-shade, in zones 5–8.

Mexican Sunflower, *Tithonia*

rotundifolia, a drought-tolerant annual, produces velvety-orange-to-scarlet flowers from July until the first frost. The leaves are velvety too. Unlike many daisylike plants, which grow in the shape of a sprawling bouquet, the Mexican sunflower shoots up to about 6 feet (although some cultivars are shorter) and stretches out airily graceful branches. All the same, the sculptural contours are weighty enough to anchor a cutting bed. Plant in well-drained soil, in full sun.

Persian Ranunculus, *Ranunculus asiaticus*, belongs to the buttercup family, though the only

obvious trait it shares with its tiny wild cousin is vibrant flower

color. Although the palette includes brassy buttercup yellow, it also encompasses shocking pink, neon orange, rice-powder white, lipstick red, and a cosmetics counter's array of rosy, creamy tones. The 3-to-5-inch-wide blooms, which appear in early summer atop stalks a foot tall or taller, recall the full skirts of exhibition ballroom dancers (they are champion cut flowers). In warm climates, Persian ranunculus is a perennial. Elsewhere, the tuberous roots must be dug up and wintered in a dry place indoors. They can be replanted in the garden in spring, after all danger of frost has passed. Plenty of sunlight and excellent drainage are essential; zones 8–10.

Purple Beauty Berry, *Callicarpa dichotoma*,

is a handsome, compact shrub (3 to 4 feet in height), which is cultivated for the profuse metallic lilac-colored fruits that encircle the stems in great, eye-popping clusters in autumn (*Callicarpa,* from the Greek for "beautiful fruit," is an understatement). The lavender flowers, a midsummer preview to the climactic berries, are a pretty bonus. Since *Callicarpa dichotoma* blooms on new growth, it should be pruned hard every spring. Plant the shrub in moist, well-drained soil, in full sun, in zones 5–8.

Red-Twig Dogwood, *Cornus sericea*,

is riveting in winter, when its array of crimson stems, ultimately 7 feet tall and upright, with a similar spread, glow against the drab brown, gray, and white of a frosty landscape. Position it with this seasonal display in mind, as an isolated specimen, as a hedge, or mixed with different trees and shrubs at the edge of a woodland garden. In spring it produces white flowers and leaves that are dark green on top, whitish underneath. Berries, which appear in summer, are white, too. Plant in consistently moist soil, in full sun or part shade, in zones 3–8.

Smoke Bush, *Cotinus coggygria* 'Royal Purple'

(*opposite*), a deciduous shrub, gets its name from the fuzzy remains of the blossoms that appear in late summer and resemble puffs of smoke against the sky. The foliage is a rich red-purple. Grown either multi-or single-stemmed, smoke bush reaches 10 to 15 feet in height, with a 10-foot spread. A lone specimen of *Cotinus coggygria* 'Royal Purple' makes an alluring focal point; a closely spaced row becomes a garden smoke screen. For optimum hazy effect, cut branches back hard each spring. The shrub adapts to many soil types but does best planted in well-drained soil, in full sun, in zones 5–8.

Threadleaf Japanese Maple,

Acer palmatum 'Dissectum' (*page 159*), is technically a tree, but because of its deeply etched leaves and graceful weeping habit, it is often used as if it were an ornamental shrub. In autumn, the green foliage turns a brilliant red, reason enough to plant one (or more). Even in a garden where flowers dominate, this Japanese maple stands out year-round; prune the branches to accentuate their delicate contours and airy canopy. Plant in soil that's moist, well drained, and high in organic matter, in full sun or light shade (sun makes the fall color dazzling), in zones 6–8.

Witch Hazel, *Hamamelis* x *intermedia*

'Arnold Promise', a vase-shaped shrub, heralds spring with yellow, fragrant flowers as early as February or the beginning of March. Because the straplike petals, an inch or so long, are impervious to frost, this shower of gold persists when there's little else to marvel at in the garden. Witch hazel is bewitching in autumn, too, when the leaves turn reddish. Maturing to a height of 15 feet or more, it likes moist, acid, well-drained soil high in organic matter and full sun to light shade, in zones 5–9.

Zinnia, *Zinnia* 'Candycane', a new cultivar (*page*

162), shows what hybridizing can do to rev up color. The original zinnias, Mexican natives that flowered in purple and yellow, were called eyesores by the Aztecs. Zinnias weren't received with much enthusiasm in Europe, either, except by nineteenth-century breeders who transformed the genus. Zinnias come in every color but blue, grow from 6 inches to 3 feet tall, and yield flowers ranging from 2 to 6 inches across. Sow seeds or plant in well-drained soil high in organic matter, allowing good air circulation to prevent (or retard) mildew, in full sun.

Leaves of the smoke bush *Cotinus coggygria* **'Royal Purple'** (*opposite*) **arch to meet the light. The smoky blossoms, not yet in full, hazy bloom, will soon cover the plant.** *Left:* **A sumptuous lettuce,** *Latuca sativa* **'Red Sails' is ornamental in garden bed and salad bowl alike.** *Above:* **Hybrid candelabra primroses,** *Primula* **spp., light up an early spring landscape.**

TEXTURE

Because color is the most obvious attraction in the landscape, an appreciation for the subtler character of texture comes later for most gardeners. But after you've set up house with certain plants for a while, you come to see them in new ways and value the textural qualities that emerge over time as strengths you can depend upon. The etching of a leaf or the filigree of twigs; the contrast of shiny foliage next to matte; shaggy bark near smooth; a fringe of reeds blurring a stone path; a lace collar of fronds softening the rim of a pool—the slightest gestures suggest roles you'll want each plant to play. Texture speaks volumes about a plant's essential personality. More to the point for garden design, it's what you will enjoy seeing and touching through the seasons, long after flowers have faded and fallen. Like brushstrokes on canvas, each plant contributes another layer to the richly varied texture of your surroundings.

In winter, dried flower spikes of feather reed grass, *Calamagrostis* x *acutiflora* 'Stricta' *(opposite)* soften a sweep of land with quill-pen strokes of light. In summer, 3-to-4-foot flower spikes rise above the stiff-edged, arching foliage at the base of the grass. *Above:* Any single leaf of lady's mantle, *Alchemilla mollis,* works its alchemy, gathering drops of rain or dew on its finely pleated surface.

Cardoon, *Cynara cardunculus*, is a formidable annual or, in the southern states, a tender perennial, with stunning jagged-edged leaves up to 3 feet long. The foliage is pewter-colored on the top, white underneath. Cardoon skyrockets 4 to 6 feet high by early summer and then sends up thick gray stems yet another couple of feet, yielding a crown of thistlelike purple flowers. Give it room to spread out, and prepare for it to dominate the scene. Plant in moist, well-drained soil high in organic matter, in full sun; hardy in zones 9 and 10.

Date Palm, *Phoenix* spp. *(page 171)*, encompasses a range of tender palms whose overlapping fronds filter sunlight like a loosely woven hat, gently shifting in the breeze. In the southernmost states, they sketch a familiar silhouette against the sky. North of the tropics, date palms are grown as winter houseplants that can happily summer outdoors. *P. dactylifera* has multiple slender trunks with gray-green waxy leaves. Plant in well-drained soil, in full sun; zones 9–11.

Egyptian Onion, *Allium cepa* (*Proliferum* group) *(page 170)*, is the plant you order for onions on the top. The entire allium genus—flowering bulbs in the lily family, which encompasses garlic and onions—was once restricted to the vegetable or herb garden, but no more. The plants are now as widely valued for the pastel fireworks of their flower clusters as they are for the flavor of their edible bulbs, notwithstanding the oniony redolence of their leaves when you rub them. With the Egyptian onion, clusters of bulblets appear to have made a wrong turn, ending up on top of 4-foot flower stalks after the bloom is spent. The stalk looks as if it's wearing a crown of braided shallots. Plant in rich, well-drained soil, in full sun, in zones 5–8.

Feather Reed Grass, *Calamagrostis* x *acutiflora* 'Stricta' *(opposite)*, looks like the product of a strict but loving home, its posture erect yet flexible enough to arch in the wind. The clumps reach 2 to 4 feet in height, and the green and pink flower spikes, which appear early in the summer, rise another 3 or 4 feet above the foliage. After drying to a soft gold in autumn, the rustling reeds wave on in the winter garden. Plant in moist, well-drained soil rich in organic matter, in full sun; zones 5–9.

Heavenly Bamboo, *Nandina domestica*,

can be counted on for unearthly beauty, either as a soft-textured focal point among other shrubs or as a border accent in summer and winter alike. Technically an evergreen, its dainty leaves (which resemble true bamboo) are blue-green in summer, then "ever-red" all winter, when heavy clusters of vivid red berries (or white or yellow, depending on the cultivar), cascade from the mounded shrub. Most cultivars grow 6 to 8 feet high, although there are some dwarfs available that top out around 2 feet. Plant in moist, well-drained soil rich in organic matter, in full sun or partial shade, in zones 6–9.

Lady's Mantle, *Alchemilla* spp. (*page 167*),

is a superb, grow-it-anywhere perennial—in a border, edging a path, as a ground cover. Although the leaves are downy, color, not texture, is the first trait you're likely to notice, since the soft green of lady's mantle foliage always looks fresh. Its textural charm requires close-up scrutiny: each leaf is indeed like a cloak or mantle, rounded, with minutely scalloped or deeply cut edges, often pleated to cup dewdrops that glimmer like beads of mercury. Where *Alchemilla* is happy (and it's not very hard to please), it will spread, sometimes jumping into gravel to take root. It produces sprays of yellow-green flowers early in summer, perfect for demitasse nosegays. Plant in moist, well-drained soil, with full sun to partial shade, in zones 3–7.

Lavender Cotton, *Santolina chamaecyparissus*,

a dense woolly herb 1 to 2 feet high, is used ornamentally in an herb garden, as edging for a border, or as a low hedge, much the way you'd use lavender. Silvery white on top, finely etched, and lacy, the foliage (for which the plant is primarily grown) is woolly underneath, somehow dense and airy at the same time, and cleanly fragrant. Tiny, curious, buttonlike yellow flowers appear in summer, which some people like and some don't. (Prune hard in spring to skip the flowers.) Plant in well-drained soil, in full sun, in zones 6–8.

Love-Lies-Bleeding, *Amaranthus caudatus*,

was a favorite of the Victorians, who adorned their gardens with its blood red, drooping flower clusters the way they festooned their sofas with tassels. A tender annual that grows like a shrub, with variations in foliage shape and flower color from cultivar to cultivar, love-lies-bleeding grows upright and spreads. For contemporary tastes, it's perhaps best considered not as a focal point but as a textural contrast, with the taillike clusters dangling in the background while other flowers reach up in the foreground. Plant in well-drained soil in full sun.

Maidenhair Fern, *Adiantum pedatum*,

presents a delicate yet shapely foil for all sorts of plants in a shady bed or a woodland glade; it is also an effective underplanting for other shrubs. Growing 1 to 2 feet high, in tight, slow-spreading clumps, this perennial (also known as five-finger fern and northern maidenhair fern) produces fan-shaped fronds that open from wiry black stems. Incandescent pale green in spring, the fronds turn a deeper blue-green over the course of the season. Plant in moist soil high in organic matter, in shade; zones 3–8.

Oakleaf Hydrangea,

Hydrangea quercifolia, is unusual among hydrangeas for its large, deep green leaves, soft as down underneath, as well as for the stately way it passes through the season. Use as a mounded hedge, in a shrubbery or border, just about anywhere. Growing typically 4 to 6 feet and spreading like a skirt, it yields its flower heads horizontally in summer, an ivory white deepening to pinkish bronze. The leaves change color in autumn as well, in a range of rich oranges to purples. Exfoliating bark provides winter interest. Plant in moist, fertile, well-drained soil, in sun to partial shade; zones 5–9.

Prickly Pear, *Opuntia* species (*opposite*),

comprises a large genus with diverse characteristics—some grow quickly, some slowly; some are covered with spines, some

Love-lies-bleeding, *Amaranthus caudatus* (*right*) trails plush tassels. *Opposite:* The aptly named prickly pear, *Opuntia,* has a tough-guy vigor that plays up the languid charms of more delicate plants.

with bristles; some are spiky and forbidding, some almost velvety. Growth habits vary from tall and cylindrical to short and spreading, and the showy, waxy flowers bloom in spring or summer in a range of colors. The berries produced are sometimes edible—these are the prickly pears you find in gourmet markets—but peel them carefully, as the fine bristles that break off can irritate the skin. Those bristles are a good reason not to plant a prickly pear anywhere you do lots of hand-weeding. Drought-tolerant once established, grouped or planted as lone specimens, *Opuntia* species create a bold, sculptural effect in the stark landscapes where they thrive. Plant in full sun to part shade; zones vary, depending on species.

Sea Holly, *Eryngium* species, works as a trusty

sidekick to soft, rounded, mounded, or spreading flowers, flowering as it does in spiky blue thistle heads above spiny bracts that look like notched collars. Not really threatening at all, sea holly is an ideal border rebel, interjecting a note of punk style among fluffy or floppy companions. It also has an ornamental place in a vegetable patch and a functional place in a cutting garden. Depending on the species, the plant attains a height of 1 to 4 feet. Plant in well-drained soil, in full sun; zones 5–8.

Sweet Iris, *Iris pallida* 'Albo-variegata',

sports stunning, variegated foliage, streaked with white and cream on a soft blue-green background. This variation on the classic iris theme dresses up a bed or a border even when the plant isn't in bloom. Intensely fragrant, pale—hence *pallida*—bluish lavender flowers with yellow-tipped beards open in late spring, on stems that rise to 3 feet tall. Sweet iris rhizomes (rootstock) are powdered for use in perfumeries. Plant in well-drained soil, in full sun; zones 5–8.

Trifoliate Orange, *Poncirus*

trifoliata, is a compelling shrub or small tree to look at, but don't touch: the narrow thorns are vicious. As a specimen, planted in a (gigantic) pot or rooted in the ground as an impenetrable hedge, this tree grows erect and rigid. The bright green thorns project from the glossy green stem or trunk in oval patterns. Small, bright green leaves emerge in spring, followed by lightly fragrant, tiny white flowers, then bitter little oranges early in the autumn. There's an admirable haughtiness to this plant and a chastening reminder that not all things in nature are cozy or cuddly. Plant in well-drained acidic soil, in full sun; zones 6–9.

Yellow Corydalis, *Corydalis lutea*, is a

diminutive perennial, no taller than a foot, that calls to mind sprites and leprechauns. In spring, the low mounds of ferny leaves—perfect for the little folk to gambol in—are canopied by tiny yellow flowers (blue in some species). The plants bloom repeatedly throughout the growing season. When corydalis is comfortable, it will self-sow its way throughout garden beds and pathways and on into sidewalk cracks and wall crevices. Plant it in fertile, well-drained soil, in full sun or (for longer, more intense blooming) partial shade, in zones 5–8.

Yucca, *Yucca* species, refined and rugged all at

once, tops the list of punctuation points in the landscape (that's how Gertrude Jekyll deployed this perennial, with a bold hand). Flanking an entrance or formal stairway, a pair of mature yuccas is as impressive as a couple of Swiss Guards. The shrubby clusters of sword-shaped leaves are evergreen; color varies according to cultivar, ranging from grayish to golden. Beware of the stiff blades' sharp tips, which can wound the unwary gardener or passerby. In summer (sometimes every other summer), stems as thick as a stout walking stick emerge from the foliage, rise to 6 feet, and explode into huge, astonishing panicles of creamy white, cupped blossoms. Plant yuccas in well-drained soil, in full sun; depending on the species, zones 5–10.

Opposite: Foliage protrudes from bulblets atop the stem of Egyptian onion, *Allium cepa* (*Proliferum* group), forming contours as sparely elegant as a tribal figurine. *Below*: The date palm, *Phoenix* spp., bursts into leafy fireworks.

CLIMBERS

Climbing plants work with the gardener to help tie the earth to the sky, lifting the landscape high into three dimensions and providing it with a luminous ceiling. Training a climber or, if it's so inclined, letting it scale the heights on its own, can be your most dramatic design gesture. This is as close as you'll come to magic tricks for softening the starkness of a wall, casting shade where there is glaring sun, screening a view that makes you wince, draping a doorway, dressing up a fence, curtaining an outdoor shower. Many climbers can't perform without human help— they need to be tied to a sturdy post or trellis; some need taut wires, strings, or even another climber to curl their tendrils around. But start a single seed of an annual vine, like morning glory, and there's no stopping its ascent. The hardest part about planting a young perennial climber is the wait. But remember the adage: First year, it sleeps; second, it creeps; third year, it leaps! After that, it's your job to keep climbers from clambering into windows and other places where they're unwelcome. Decisive pruning is a hard but necessary lesson for eager gardeners to learn. Then, the sky's the limit.

Climbing roses such as 'New Dawn' (*opposite*) **are actually shrubs that will flourish aloft only when their long canes are attached to a solid support.** *Above:* **Bougainvillea, a shrubby vine, happily scales any structure within reach.**

Boston Ivy, *Parthenocissus tricuspidata* (*page 176*), gave Boston's brick walls an air of venerability long before they were old enough to warrant it (and despite its name, it's a native of Asia, not New England). The stems will grow in whichever direction they're pointed until they come across something to climb, at which time the ivy produces convenient little rootlets that grab on to just about any surface. From the instant the ascent (or the descent or lateral creep) begins, the plant's tenacity is amazing. No wonder it can hide, or enhance, any problem wall or corner of the garden. The three-lobed leaves are deciduous, turning orange-red to coincide with the back-to-school season. Adaptable to most sites, even urban conditions, it will grow in sun or shade, in zones 4–8.

Bougainvillea (*page 172*), available as various hybrids, is a tender climber that grows vigorously, even rampantly. Bright, colorful bracts (modified leaves), which have the translucency and texture of fine paper, virtually enclose the inconspicuous flowers. This climber is most famous for its magenta bracts, but it also comes in yellow, white, and orange. Bougainvillea grows in a swath across the southern states, where it is de rigueur as a living curtain to shade porches and pergolas. A woody, thorny, ungainly plant that tends to ramble and sprawl, it requires a firm structure to grip and firm pruning to keep it in line. Once established, bougainvillea is drought-tolerant. This plant needs well-drained soil and full sun; zones 10 and 11.

Clematis comprises more than 200 species and many more hybrids. With careful planning, you can have a sequence of clematis in bloom all season long, trailing over and through fences and arbors and around and among shrubs and trees. They climb by means of twining leaf stalks that need to be guided during the ascent. The range of flower size, form, color, and period of bloom is extraordinary. One of the easiest to grow is sweet autumn clematis, *C. paniculata*, which produces clouds of small, white, fragrant flowers in late summer, and reaches 25 feet in a few seasons. Colorful, large-flowered hybrids bloom in summer and fall, and ramble pleasingly through hedges and shrubs. In general, clematis likes its roots shaded by mulch or by lower-growing plants. The plant wants moist, well-drained soil and sun or partial shade, depending on the species or cultivar; zones 4–8.

Climbing Hydrangea,

Hydrangea anomala ssp. *petiolaris*, takes a while to get established. Once settled in, though, it's a climber out of a fairy tale castle. The foliage is shiny and dark green, the perfect foil for the huge, gorgeous clusters of ivory white blooms in June and July. Once this deciduous plant sheds its leaves, the sinuous branches trace calligraphic flourishes against the wall, their bark peeling like cinnamon. Provide moist, well-drained soil high in organic matter and full sun or partial shade; zones 5–7.

Climbing Roses, *Rosa* hybrids (*page 172*),

grow exuberantly, lending an air of classic, sensuous elegance to any structure they're attached to. Walk through an arbor with rose petals falling gently around you, and you'll be hooked for life. In all its many forms, *Rosa* is a woody shrub with sprawling canes that aren't self-supporting but can readily be attached with string or rope to posts, arbors, gates, or walls. The plants bloom lavishly early in the summer, some continuously or intermittently throughout the summer, depending on the species or cultivar you choose—and there are dozens upon dozens to choose from in countless colors and a bewildering range of categories (*e.g.*, both climbers *and* ramblers), some fragrant, some not. They need moist, well-drained soil rich in organic matter and full sun. Depending on the species or cultivar, roses thrive in zones 3–9.

Dutchman's Pipe, *Aristolochia*

macrophylla, got its name because as the petalless calyx emerges into bloom, the greenish flower resembles a pipe, though why a Dutchman's is anyone's guess. Deciduous and vigorous, it makes a fine cover-up in full leaf. Until they fall in the autumn, the broad, heart-shaped leaves furnish a soothing backdrop for colorful borders or shrubs. The vine grows easily in moist, well-drained soil and in full sun to partial shade; zones 4–7.

Passion flower, *Passiflora* sp. (*above*), blooms into intricate whirligigs. *Right*: The blossom of goldflame honeysuckle, *Lonicera* x *heckrottii*, seems to hover above its foliage like a dragonfly. *Opposite*: Within a summer's span, the rapid growth of morning glory *Ipomoea tricolor* 'Heavenly Blue' is an annual miracle.

Goldflame Honeysuckle,

Lonicera x *heckrottii (below)*, is so prolific that you can let it go for a luxuriantly wild tangle or prune it for a more domesticated display. A sturdy vine, it twines freely on any structure you put it near and has an exceptionally long blooming period, from late spring through early summer, then sporadically into the fall. The delicate blossoms flame golden at first, then fade to the softer hues of sunrise. The contrasting leaves are a dark blue-green, with purple-red stems. The plants need moist, well-drained, slightly acidic soil and full sun; zones 5–9.

Hops, *Humulus lupulus*, a perennial herb, is far more

common in Britain than it is here (except where it is harvested for the bitter-tasting flower clusters used in brewing beer). That is a pity, because we have just as much to hide, and few living things conceal an eyesore faster. Hops need support but they grow rapidly—as much as 30 feet in a single year. The deep-lobed leaves play nicely with sunlight; the pale green conical bracts and flowers do, too, but only in the female plant. Needs moist, well-drained soil and full sun; zones 4–8.

Hyacinth Bean, *Lablab purpurea*, also

known as *Dolichos lablab*, is a vine show in three acts. Act one is the emergence of leaves, which are an unusual deep purplish green. Act two is the bloom of clustered lavender flowers. Act three features showy glossy purple seedpods that look as if they've been polished to a satiny sheen (the pods, or beans, are eaten in the tropics, where they are a staple legume; here, their value is ornamental). A striking contrast to any mass of greenery, hyacinth bean twines its way up a trellis or post. It needs moist, well-drained soil and full sun, and it actually does best in the heat of summer; perennial in zones 10 and 11, annual elsewhere.

Japanese Wisteria, *Wisteria*

floribunda, pumps out masses of long, pendulous, violet flower clusters—as big as bunches of grapes—in late spring, with a heady fragrance that promises undying romance. The twining vine is woody and deciduous. After you plant a Japanese wisteria, it will probably take a few years to bloom profusely, but it's worth the wait. And as the vine ages, the stems turn into smooth, serpentine trunks that wind around their supports. Make sure that those supports are robust enough (4 x 4 timbers are none too thick) to withstand wisteria's boa constrictor grip. It asks for moist, well-drained soil high in organic matter and full sun; zones 4–9.

Kolomikta Kiwi, *Actinidia kolomikta*,

lures you with its leaves, which start out bronze in the spring, when everything else is pale green, then blur to a spattering of pink and white that, from a distance, looks deceptively like flower petals (in fact, tiny clusters of white blooms do appear in spring). A twining vine, kiwi needs some structure to support it, and will eventually reach about 15 feet. In order for it to yield fruit, both a male and a female plant must be present. Curiously, cats love rubbing against the bark; to protect this vulnerable coating, wrap it in burlap or landscape cloth until the vine is well established. Average garden soil is all it needs, in full sun to partial shade; zones 4–8.

Morning Glory, *Ipomoea tricolor (page 175)*,

actually stays glorious all day, or at least until the sun grows hot enough to wilt it. This annual vine is a member of the *Convolvulaceae* family, whose name derives from the Latin for "entwine." Use your fingertips to guide the slender stems and petioles around taut string, wire, a fence post, or whatever else you want it to coil around, and watch this prodigious climber grow, sometimes by the hour. Trumpet-shaped blue, rose, or white blossoms appear all summer up till the frost, beginning in July. Give it well-drained soil and full sun.

Passion Flower, *Passiflora (page 174)*

in its various species, is the Armani of vines—a tropical or subtropical native with large, distinctive, complex, yet exquisitely restrained blossoms you recognize at a glance. The plant twines readily and, in the warmer zones where it is hardy, the leaves are semi- to evergreen. Elsewhere, it is treated as an annual. They prefer moist, well-drained soil high in organic matter and full sun to partial shade; zones 8–11.

Poet's Jasmine, *Jasminum officinale*,

also known as common jasmine, is technically not a vine at all, but a shrub that can be trained as a climber. Guide it up a trellis, and you'll never know the difference. The dark leaves are semi-evergreen, but it's the legendary fragrant white flower clusters, blooming during the summer, that make Yankees dream of moving south. This jasmine asks for moist, well-drained soil and full sun to partial shade; zones 8–10.

Silverlace Vine, *Fallopia aubertii*,

or *Polygonum aubertii*, is also commonly known as the mile-a-minute vine, which gives you an idea of its growth rate.

Like an instant privacy screen, this speedy deciduous vine spreads over fences, verandas, and walls, and—if you aren't fast enough to keep up—it'll fling itself across roofs, looking in no time as if it's been around forever (in fact, it originated in China and Tibet). Zillions of minute white flowers cover the vine like a mantilla, from July through September. It adapts to most sites and needs full sun; zones 4–8.

Trumpet Vine, *Campsis radicans*,

redeems that old cliché, the clinging vine. Also known as trumpet creeper, it comes to life in midsummer with lovely funnel-shaped flowers, orange, yellow, or scarlet, depending on the cultivar you choose. Hummingbirds love its nectar. You need heavy supports for trumpet vine, since it's an obstreperous climber (by the same token, it's a quick cover-up for problem areas). Rootlike holdfasts cling by themselves, and the vine needs frequent pruning to keep it in bounds. Tolerant of most soils, it requires full sun; zones 4–9.

Virginia Creeper, *Parthenocissus quinquefolia*,

is a fast-growing deciduous vine with soft green five-leaflet foliage (each leaf resembles a little hand) that turns crimson in the autumn. Fall's crop of blue berries is irresistible to birds. The creeper climbs by branching tendrils with adhesive tips, like suction cups; wield clippers to keep them from latching on to wood shingles or clapboard. Tolerates any soil or conditions and grows in sun or shade, in zones 3–9.

The white flowers of silverlace vine, *Polygonum aubertii* (*above*), nearly conceal the plant's own foliage as well as the arbor it entwines. *Opposite: What* brick wall? Boston ivy, *Parthenocissus tricuspidata*, makes short work of even the most imposing masonry. *Left:* Intoxicatingly fragrant flower clusters of Japanese wisteria, *Wisteria floribunda*, are a springtime distraction from the killer grip of the woody vine's main stem.

SPREADERS

The words "ground cover" have the connotation of a horticultural afterthought, ho-hum plants to roll out by the yard when there's leftover space to fill. Wrong. Plants that spread and creep, making their way under, around, and between things ought to suggest a richly figured carpet, not monochrome wall-to-wall hi-lo pile. Spreaders are matchmakers in the garden, giving the visitor a reason to linger over the fine points

of each plant without ignoring the aesthetic liaisons that bind one plant to another. Whether they rise only inches off the ground or stand several feet high, spreaders are the plants to rely on for edging beds and borders, lining paths, relieving the monotony of a stone or brick terrace, mediating between woodland and lawn (now *there's* a spreader that's sometimes more trouble than it's worth). "Underplanting," like "prostrate," is another word with overtones of low esteem, but the lower a garden starts, and the sooner it starts to spread, the deeper the pleasure it offers. Spreaders spread in all sorts of ways (rhizomes, runners, and self-seeding, to name a few), each at its own pace. Let the race begin.

Blue Star Creeper, *Pratia pedunculata* or *Laurentia fluviatilis*, spreads out a dense, soft mat of delicate gray-green leaves, which seem to hold the light. In summer, whitish blue, or bluish white, starlike flowers hover above the foliage. It's useful among masonry pavers, in a rock garden, or as edging for a grouping of shrubs. Plenty of moisture is essential, along with well-drained soil high in organic matter, and full sun to partial shade; zones 7 and 8.

Blue Rug Juniper, *Juniperus horizontalis* 'Wiltonii', lays down a serene, extraordinarily flat carpet just 4 to 6 inches high, but 6 to 8 feet wide. The foliage is silvery blue with a light purplish cast in winter. It's true that the prostrate junipers have long been landscapers' shrubs of choice for commercial and institutional settings, but don't blame the plant for the banal results. In a domestic garden, used judiciously, the blue rug can add ground-level luxury to a grouping of shrubs, or, in an expanse of lawn, suggest a magical pool of foliage. Plus they protect problem areas like hillsides and banks from erosion. They need only well-drained soil and full sun; zones 3–9.

Creeping Thyme, *Thymus serpyllum*, is the herb that gardeners dream about stepping on, both for its cushiony softness underfoot and for the fragrance it releases. Besides fulfilling that fantasy, creeping thyme fills in the cracks on a terrace or lines the edge of a bed. The aromatic, dark green leaves grow 3 to 6 inches high, and, in midsummer, minuscule pinkish purple flowers glimmer subtly amid the foliage, rather than above it. This perennial likes well-drained soil and full sun; zones 5–9.

European Wild Ginger, *Asarum europeum,* hugs the ground with 3-inch-wide, heart-shaped leaves so glossy they look as if they've just been buffed. Because the foliage is evergreen, it earns its keep in the garden all year long. The brownish purple flowers are insignificant—or at least inconspicuous, since they lurk under the foliage. Ginger is a bit slow to spread, but even before filling out, it provides a wonderful textural counterpoint to fellow shade lovers like ferns and hostas. It's not very heat-tolerant, so keep it moist in well-drained, acidic soil rich in organic matter; zones 4–8.

A freshet of blue star creeper, *Pratia pedunculata* (*left*), flows through and around a stepping-stone stairway, as if lighting the way for safe passage. *Opposite*: Undaunted by dry shade, hardy cyclamen creeps through fallen leaves on the floor of a woodland garden.

Hardy Cyclamen, *Cyclamen* spp.

(*page 178*), is best planted under shrubs or in a woodland garden, and will self-seed. The leaves are green with silvery patterns that seem to light up dark areas, and the flower stalks coil like springs when seed capsules develop. Bloom time depends on the species, and the blossoms can be white or various shades of pink. The ideal soil is well drained but moist, though never soggy, and high in organic matter; plants should be given partial shade; zones 6–9.

Ice Plant, *Delosperma cooperi*, its name

notwithstanding, is a succulent from South Africa. Even so, it has proved surprisingly hardy farther north; it will spread, trail, or cascade, depending on where you set it down. The foliage is bluish, spangled with low, 2-inch pinkish purple flowers from summer into fall. The soil must be perfectly well drained and the plant needs full sun; zones 5–9.

Japanese Anemone, *Anemone*

tomentosa, looks, through most of the season, like a low (2 or 3 feet tall) handsome mound, with deeply lobed dark green leaves. From late summer into early fall, however, dusty mauve pink flowers rise above the foliage and dance in the wind. It spreads comfortably to form colonies in moist, well-drained soil, and flourishes in light shade to full sun (if kept moist); zones 4–8.

Myrtle, or periwinkle, *Vinca minor*, shines almost

anywhere, being a lustrous but tough plant that faithfully sends out runners. It's evergreen, too, so it textures the snow in winter. The always dapper 3- to 6-inch-high mat of leaves shows off small, neat flowers in blue, white, or violet, depending on the cultivar. Myrtle needs well-drained soil rich in organic matter, and full sun to light shade; zones 4–8.

Plumbago, or leadwort, *Ceratostigma*

plumbaginoides, gets off to a slow start, with foliage emerging in late spring (the delay makes it fine camouflage for the yellowing foliage of early bulbs). This shining green mat, about 8 inches high, works well at the front of the border, edging shrubs, or trailing over anything low. In late summer, intense gentian blue flowers pop, and remain till the leaves begin to turn a smoldering crimson that lasts well into fall. Requires well-drained soil with full sun to partial shade; zones 5–8.

Spotted Nettle, *Lamium*

maculatum (*below*), is decorative enough for a formal border, yet sufficiently relaxed for a woodland glade. It puts forth runners to spread vigorously. The silvery, heart-shaped foliage, which gleams in dappled light, grows about a foot high. Pretty white or yellow flowers appear in spring. *Lamium* flourishes in moist, well-drained soil and partial shade; zones 4–8.

Stonecrop Sedum, *Sedum*

kamtschaticum, is a succulent that sprawls in all directions, at a gentle, leisurely pace. Once established, stonecrop, like most of its sedum brethren, is remarkably accommodating, demands little care, and holds its own on erosion-prone banks and hillsides. Flower clusters, 6 inches tall, are a summer bonus. Needs well-drained soil and full sun; zones 3–9.

Sweet Woodruff, *Galium odoratum*,

is an exquisitely lush, gentle-looking herb that spreads diligently, even aggressively, by crawling and creeping. Its whorls of leaves, a lime green in spring deepening to dark green over the course of the summer, yield tiny white flowers in April and May. The flowers, redolent of newly mown hay, are used to flavor May wine or to scent sachets for linens. Plant in moist, well-drained soil high in organic matter, in partial shade or full shade (in southernmost regions); zones 3–8.

Pinwheels of sweet woodruff, *Galium odoratum (above)*, spin an airy mantilla over ground in dappled shade. Tiny white flowers twinkle above the foliage in spring. *Opposite*: Green all season long, and flowering in midsummer, stonecrop sedum, *Sedum kamtschaticum*, battles erosion on a sunny, rock-bound bank. *Left*: Even when the spotted nettle *Lamium maculatum* 'White Nancy' is not in bloom, its silvery, green-etched leaves illuminate shady patches of the garden.

BINATIONS

"What goes with what?" is the eternal question for gardeners trying to master design and horticultural complexity. Unlike, for example, choosing fabrics for drapery—pulling bolt upon bolt down from the shelves to see how various colors, patterns, and weaves work together to transform a room—you can't just scrutinize swatches and make a garden. Drapery fabrics don't stop flowering; or die back, or double in size, or need dry shade, or full sun in order to thrive. To determine which plants work well together, you've got to: (1) almost forget about the flowers and focus on the foliage, and (2) determine each plant's growing habits, preferred habitat, and cultural requirements. At the nursery, it's not just about pulling one plant from row A, one from row B, then deciding if they'll look good together. Say, for example, you fall hard for poppies in glorious bloom. "How wonderfully they'll set off the *Perovskia*, that feathery lavender Russian sage," you're thinking. Yeah, for about a minute. The poppies will have come and gone so fast—flowers, first, then foliage, too—that the combination in your mind never had a chance. Think of flowers like jewelry—accessories that embellish the basics, but are baubles without them. Foliage color, texture, and the plant's underlying structure are what matter. Look hard at the mass and contours that workhorse shrubs provide, see a single tree as living sculpture, learn to prize the garden's diplomats, the grays and the chartreuses, and discover how they can, over time, link unrelated areas in design détente.

Unifying focus One eye-catching plant, strategically linked to a man-made structure, can prevent chaos amid a lush, multi-colored bed. Thanks to its vigorous hold on a gate post, and its mesmerizing lavender blue flowers, the *Clematis* 'Will Goodwin' in Carol Mercer's Long Island garden (*at center, left*), prevents prima donnas on both sides of the fence from stealing the show. The balance could easily have tipped either to the bright red, flat-topped Maltese cross, *Lychnis chalcedonica,* on the right, or to the acid yellow spiky Carolina lupine, *Thermopsis villosa,* on the left. Instead, the garden maintains its equilibrium, and the gate leads to alluring spectacles whichever way a visitor turns.

Cool harmony

Amid sun-baked, arid western terrain (*left*), a ripple of crisply sculptural shapes and cool colors has a refreshing underwater feel to it, as if it were a coral reef raised from the sea. The low-growing succulents *Senecio mandraliscae,* with its spreading blue-gray foliage, and *Echeveria elegans,* or hen-and-chicks, which forms tight clumps of pale olive rosettes, are trusty edging plants in many drought-tolerant gardens, or Xeriscapes. Here the succulents edge together, encroaching on each other's territory to heighten the textural counterpoint.

Color clash

Deck out a border in dress-for-disaster shades, and stand back to enjoy the excitement. So long as they're matched in intensity, wildly different colors bring a whole garden alive. *Right*: Purple 'Red Giant' Asian mustard greens smolder between the molten golds of Siberian wallflower (which is anything but), *Erysimum* 'Orange Bedder', and California poppy, *Eschscholzia californica.* Without the billowing purple, the yellows and oranges would fuse into a shapeless glaring hot spot. In a far subtler contrast of hue and texture, the coarse purple mustard greens bring out the fine-toothed deep blue-green poppy foliage.

Silver threads

Gray foliage is a classic means for weaving disparate plants together or for embroidering go-with-everything trim. Here (*left*), the velvety gray leaves and flower stalks of lamb's ears, *Stachys byzantina*, coordinates with the yellowish hues of lady's mantle, *Alchemilla mollis*, in the foreground, as well as with the rosy spires of a 'Russell Hybrid' lupine (an extravagant accent plant, suited to any number of combinations, but short-lived in areas warmer than zone 6). Without the silvery band, the lady's mantle might look jaundiced against the berry pink lupine, and the lupine shrill.

Whiteout   All-white

borders like this (*right*) have been a fixation among garden designers since the turn of the century. The American writer Louise Beebe Wilder remarked on the trend more than a decade before the English writer Vita Sackville-West started her now iconic White Garden at Sissinghurst. White flowers (and white or creamy streaks in variegated foliage) reflect sunlight throughout the day; at dusk, they appear to radiate luminosity. Here, a hosta with white-etched foliage seems to support a parade of late-blooming tulips, each strong enough in spirit and habit to be visually distinct: (*left to right*) 'Snow Peak', a Darwin hybrid; 'White Dream', a Triumph hybrid; and 'Mount Tacoma', a late double. Below is an impressionist dotting of self-sowing white forget-me-nots, *Myosotis sylvatica* 'Victoria Alba'. Cascading down from above is the fragrant shrub *Viburnum* x *burkwoodii*, with spherical flower heads that are pinkish while in bud and pure white when open. Everywhere else is green.

Tapestry

Many gardeners plant beds of mixed annuals with a scattershot, laissez-faire approach, taking it for granted that the result will be a spontaneous tapestry of color. Sadly, though, when they are given free rein to shoot up, sprawl, and mingle, too many annuals just seem jumbled. Here, however, in the garden of Robert Jakob and David White, a predominant yellow-and-blue color scheme—golden *Cosmos sulphureus*, which grows 2 to 3 feet high, and cerulean *Salvia uglinosa*, 4 or 5 feet tall—gives the tapestry a loose but organizing pattern. Perennial wandflower, *Gaura lindheimeri* (*left*), keeps the bed grounded, its arching stems bearing white flowers over a long blooming season on wandlike stems; the flowers eventually fade to pink, from late summer well into the fall.

189

Fireworks For sheer razzle-dazzle, nothing beats a flash of swordlike foliage and hot-colored flowers. *Left:* In the 17,000-square-foot border at the Bellevue Botanical Garden, near Seattle, the summer spectacle includes crimson *Crocosmia x crocosmiiflora* 'Emberglow', the orange red hot–poker *Kniphofia* 'Alcazar', and the red-and-yellow daylily *Hemerocallis* 'Sherwood Chief'.

Contrast A dramatic shift from light to dark draws attention to a landscape's focal points. Both the glow and the shadow can be created with contrasting colors. *Right:* The gold of creeping Jennie, *Lysimachia nummularia* 'Aurea', is startlingly luminous amid a deep purple ring of barberry, *Berberis thunbergii* 'Crimson Pigmy', in the Bellevue border.

PLANNING THE WHOLE GARDEN

5

An arched window
in fashion designer
Linda Allard's
Connecticut pool
pavilion deliberately
frames a lush
crab apple tree
and a well-sited,
weathered bench.

I KNOW A CERTAIN GARDEN WELL, and a lot of by-the-book planning, not to mention money, went into creating it. The beds are built up, edges bricked; slopes have been leveled, the arbor is teeming with roses, and the man-made pond has a perfectly still, glassy surface. Yet you survey this perfection from a narrow terrace at the back of the house—the garden is too far away to beckon you, too far removed for you to touch. There's nothing exactly the matter with this garden; in fact, it's very well executed. But it is curiously impersonal, a garden that tells you nothing about the gardener, holds no secrets, has no plot. It's like a tastefully furnished model house; you feel that nobody really inhabits it.

Far more satisfying than this designer-perfect garden is one that springs directly from the imagination into the soil, a garden as uniquely yours as your fingerprint. Messier, perhaps, but exuberant, too. Or as restrained, restful, stimulating, cluttered, spare, manicured, formal or not, as you choose to make it. Designing your space means reflecting on your own memories and desires, and deliberately creating a place in which your soul will feel at peace. If, as a child, you loved being with your grandfather in his orchard, for example, plant a small grove of fruit trees in your own garden; they will bring that memory to life. If your family rented a wonderful old cottage at the seashore every August, when blue hydrangeas were in bloom on every street, or so it seemed, you can plant that memory permanently with a few hydrangeas of your own. You can plant desire—the rose garden down the street that you can only peek at through the fence. Or control—an herb garden with every plant in its place.

The gardens presented in this chapter range from contemplative to ebullient, walled to woodland, courtyards to country acreage. They encompass a wide spectrum of approaches to a variety of landscapes. While they all follow precisely the givens of garden design (they assemble, in fact, ideas about the five senses, the essential design elements and numerous plant choices we've detailed in the previous chapters) they interpret these givens very differently. What these gardens have in common is the personal, intimate desire of their creators for gardens that express who they are, how they want to live outdoors, and what they want the land to do—whether it's to yield vegetables for eating and flowers for cutting, to provide a haven from the world outside it, to frame the outside world and draw it in, or transform the land they have into the place they want.

These gardens aren't meant to be step-by-step templates to copy on your own plot, but rather springboards to stimulate your imagination, show what's possible, highlight a sensibility. Let the gardens that don't move you (and some won't) help you with the editing process by showing you what you don't want in your own place. Use these gardens as a checklist. Let's say you see a wall, or a fountain, or an arbor, that might look wonderful at the back of your garden. Now ask yourself: Is it the right height? What else could it be made of? How could I site it on my own land? What could I grow around it?

If you like the feel of a garden in Los Angeles, but live in New England, think how you could reinterpret it with suitable regional plants; if you're drawn to a rustic bridge but have no water, maybe a rustic arch or arbor could give a similar feeling. Or maybe you like the idea of a courtyard (or of raised beds or a garden shed). Take a moment to ask yourself the questions that every good garden designer asks: What problems does this landscape feature solve? How does it affect light and shadow? What is the ratio of structure to plants? What are its different levels (the terrace above a low wall, the rafters of a pergola, the floor of a pool)? What role do the plants play? And what feelings do those plants evoke? Are there shrubs, mostly, or flowers, too? How is the space accessorized? Is there too much stuff for you? What makes it feel comfortable? What mood does it convey and how does it convey it?

Style in the garden comes from your answers to those questions—your personal mix and match of options. Imprinted with your own memories and longings, they can grow in your garden, too.

At first glance, this looks like a typical American front yard that has been that way for years. Then, you discover that nothing here has happened by accident. To convey proper proportion, interior designer Albert Hadley's fine eye has realigned steps, redrawn the front walk, even releveled the contours of the ground.

A plan for stylish country living

THE HOUSE MAY LOOK ITALIAN, the parterre and potager French, the lawns and arbors English—but Linda Allard's garden is also grounded in Doylestown, Ohio, where Ellen Tracy's vastly successful design director first learned how to sew, and how to grow. The two pursuits, fashion and fashioning gardens, share many goals: color and texture, practicality, craftsmanship and fit, plus embellishing the classic with style. Lots of it. Allard's garden skims the land like a beautifully tailored suit, and the label is distinctly hers.

The eldest of six children, Allard grew up working in her parents' garden and in summer, on her uncle's farm; when she was ten, her mother, a 4-H advisor, taught her to sew. After graduating from college in 1962, she boarded a Greyhound bus for New York with only $200 in her pocket, found a job with a then-tiny company, and quickly worked her way up. Now, of the three Ellen Tracy lines she designs, one label bears her name as well. As for gardening, Allard bought a tiny house in the Connecticut woods and spent twenty years in the shade and between the roots. Longing for sun, sky, and open spaces, she eventually bought 55 acres—rolling hills with spectacular views—and decided to build her own house. She collaborated with her brother David, an architect, on the house and, from the beginning, included the gardens she wanted in their plan. Landscape designer Bob Zion was responsible for big-picture elements such as sculpting an entryway and terracing lawns into a ha-ha to keep the deer out. Allard and her brother, however, designed the actual gardens: the pool garden, with lavender and roses, tucked behind sandblasted concrete walls, a boxwood parterre, a series of rose arbors, and a vegetable garden, Allard's special province, with borders of tulips, iris, peonies, white lilies, and delphinium.

Even before the house was completed, Allard planned the garden, trying the spaces on for size the way she might drape fabric on a dressmaker's form. She sees gardening—again like fashion—as a process of evolution. "I like to experiment. The first couple of years I had beans where the boxwood would go; my rose arbors were once tomatoes on stakes. I tried morning glories where I eventually put my standard-trained roses. That made it easier for me to work out a sense of proportion. A packet of seeds doesn't cost very much, so planting annuals is a great way to get a feel for the shapes, and to make sure you like it all before you put in perennials and permanent structures. And we did make changes, like widening the path beneath the arbors by two feet."

IN THE PLANNING STAGE,
REMEMBER THAT YOUR FLAT
SKETCH MUST WORK IN THREE
DIMENSIONS. *Height is one design
variable that often gets lost in the shuffle,
but it imparts an exciting, multilayered
feel to Linda Allard's vegetable garden.
Sandblasted concrete walls (ranging
from 4 to 8 feet tall, and home to more
than fifty varieties of espaliered apples)
provide lasting vertical drama. Other
upwardly mobile players—like towering
sunflowers and bamboo tepees covered
in scarlet runner beans and 'Early
Cascade' and 'Champion' tomatoes—
change positions from year to year.*

199

AN EXACT STYLE MATCH
CAN SEEM CLOYING OR
STIFF, BUT A HOUSE AND
ITS GARDEN SHOULD LIVE
TOGETHER COMFORTABLY.
*Linda Allard and her architect-
brother David began work on
this garden while they were
designing the house. So it's no
surprise that inside and out join
seamlessly. Every window frames
a view; the walled garden (which
contains the potager, parterre,
and rose arbors) flows from the
east axis of the house; the pool
garden and courtyard flank the
west wing. But the Allards knew
better than to re-create an
Italian landscape for the Tuscan-
and Palladian-inspired house.
Instead, they designed an
original garden that—with its
classic European style, formal
symmetry, and sandstone-colored
hardscaping—compliments, but
never mimics, the architecture.*

Surprisingly, now that they're established, the central rose arbors, the parterre, and the pool garden are fairly low-maintenance. Allard has a caretaker to help, which leaves her free to spend her weekends in the vegetable garden, a domain where ornamental beauty and edible bounty coexist to supply the house with food and flowers, and to supply the soul with the nourishment it needs. This garden is a year-round venture. Allard thinks it through when the seed catalogs arrive each January ("It changes every year; with vegetables, you have to rotate the crops"), starts seedlings in her conservatory come February, and harvests the last of the root vegetables in December.

Allard experimented with space here, too. Since most of these vegetables and flowers are annuals, she simply tested them in different patterns for a couple of years until she hit on the right one. Only then did Allard sod some paths and pave others with sandstone, brought in from Ohio. "Once you put in stone," she laughs, "you're pretty committed." The pathways keep track of rows and rows of vegetables, which become softly impressionistic when abundant flowers are mixed in. In addition to the garden walls, tepees for beans and tomatoes add verticality. An eighteenth-century English sundial centers one half of the vegetable garden; a French statue divides the other. The ensemble is intricate and complex yet never overbearing, because of the for-

Allard relaxes in the pool pavilion with her brother David, his wife, Gloria, and their children, Rachel and David.

stylish country living

mal simplicity of the arbors that separate potager from parterre, the serene splash of water flowing from a Roman rainspout mounted on a wall, the reflective quiet of the pool garden nearby, and the calm sweep of undulating hills all around.

"Vegetables are so beautiful," Allard says, "even before you mix in herbs and flowers. Last year, I planted by color: purple beds with purple eggplants, purple flowers, purple peppers. Then I had yellow peppers, yellow tomatoes, yellow flowers. It was fun, doing color boxes." Texture is also a preoccupation: "Combining color and texture—it's the same process I go through when I'm doing clothes." Indeed, some of Allard's combinations suggest a horticultural layered look: the crinkly blue-green leaves of Savoy cabbages with the yellow flowers of ferny dill and blue cornflowers, bright red tomatoes with deep scarlet runner beans, chartreuse leeks with dark blue *Salvia farinacea* 'Victoria', poppies among the asparagus.

Allard, who likes to cook and has written a cookbook, *Absolutely Delicious!*, also appreciates the continuity of the growing cycle, the functional nature of her garden, and the way it reminds her of her childhood home in Ohio. "I've traveled a lot, and my taste has changed over the years. But basically, I still grow what my father did: onions, peas, potatoes, tomatoes, all that stuff." The same sensibility that she imparts to her clothes? Sure. "It's practical. You use it. But it's also great-looking."

203

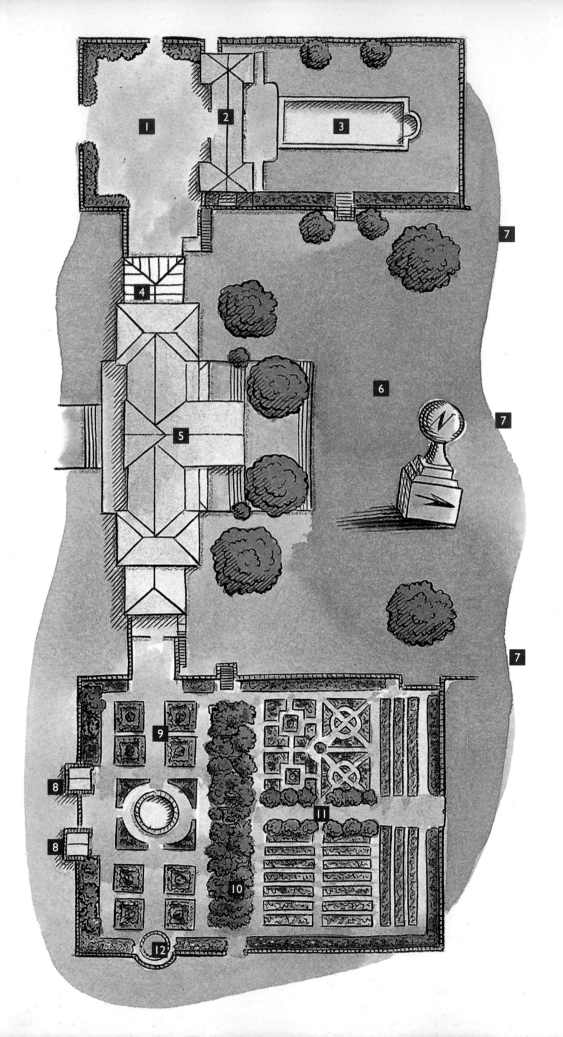

PLAN KEY

True to the classical style of the house, all garden areas have been clustered within two rectangles, as if they are wings symmetrically flanking the central building. This is a basic layout in Palladian architecture, which has inspired American design since the Colonial era.

1 COURTYARD

2 POOL PAVILION

3 POOL

4 CONSERVATORY

5 HOUSE

6 BACK LAWN

7 HA-HA

8 POTTING SHEDS

9 ROSE AND BOXWOOD PARTERRE

10 ROSE ARBORS

11 POTAGER

12 FOUNTAIN

IN A LARGE GARDEN, SIMPLE REPETITIONS LINK THE WHOLE AND HAVE A CALMING EFFECT.

In a garden this vast, one arbor might look dinky and out of place. But fourteen of them—one after another after another— make a bold yet soothing statement. Wrapped in pink and white roses and clematis, and underplanted with lavender, Allard's wrought-iron arches (number 10 on plan, left) form a cool, shady gallery through the center of the walled garden. This path is the perfect transition between the kitchen garden and the more formal box and rose parterre.

EVEN SMALL CONTAINERS ADD BIG INTEREST TO OUTDOOR BEDS. There's no need to relegate potted plants to the living room, front porch, or patio. Besides using tepees, arbors, antique ornaments, and tall plants, Allard relies on container gardening to provide structure, vary the height, and add a bit of decoration to the garden. **Left:** *A simple terra-cotta pot, planted with geraniums and variegated ivy, anchors and enlivens a square lettuce and kale patch.*

A PROFUSION OF PLANTS KEEPS A FORMAL GARDEN FAR FROM STUFFY. This potager is strictly divided into 14 rectangular beds and 4 highly patterned squares. But Allard packs that structure full of plants—and the resulting potager is anything but manicured. Leeks, 'Lemon Gem' marigolds, tomatoes, and sunflowers escape the boundaries of their rectangular beds and spill out onto a sandstone path.

CONSIDER FORM—NOT JUST COLOR AND TEXTURE—WHEN SELECTING AND GROUPING PLANTS. *True, the spiky foliage of oriental chives is a wonderful contrast to 'The Fairy' rose's smooth oval leaves. And yes, the deep pinks and mauves blend together beautifully. But there are other, more subtle and playful, combinations here* (left). *Notice how the lollipop shape of the standard-trained roses is repeated, in miniature, through the flowering chives and how those shapes flip the silhouette of an eighteenth-century English sundial upside down.*

PROPERLY INTEGRATED, A POOL NEEDN'T BE A BLIGHT ON THE LANDSCAPE. *This is a rare sight: a swimming pool that's as beautiful as it is useful. Instead of rough, drab concrete, sandstone tiles serve as reminders of the house's exterior and the garden paths and walls. A gentle curve at the end of the pool (which cups a hot tub) gives it the same classical look. And the black bottom emits no eerie blue light. Furthermore, since the edge of the lawn is terraced into a ha-ha, the pool appears to fall away gracefully into the rolling hills beyond.*

DESIGNING WITH PATTERN

Throughout landscape history, garden makers have sketched patterns on the earth: fields of food crops set in rows, Egyptian groves with straight paths, Roman courtyards, Persian retreats, medieval cloister garths—all reflected the urge to shape nature to the human need for order. The repeated figures soothe us and tell us where to look and to walk; they also link indoors to out and make the garden feel unified. A pattern is also a starting point, a guide for placing paths, carving beds, and choosing plants. A single well-placed axis adds logic to the landscape; add crossed axes, with a fountain at the intersection, and you've re-created a Persian "paradise" court.

Patterns in paths and beds have many practical purposes as well: they provide easy access for watering and weeding, ensure that plants get maximum exposure to sun, improve drainage or water retention, and provide a simple system for keeping track of crop rotation.

Choosing the right design usually begins with a consideration of the style of your house. A geometric layout with plenty of straight lines partners well with a classical building, whether it's 1830s Greek Revival, 1920s Spanish Revival, or 1990s Contractor's Colonial; curves go with less formal styles, such as 1840s Gothic Revival, 1950s Modernistic, and 1980s neo–Shingle Style; but exceptions abound. Patterned beds make their point more clearly if they are planted simply, in massed groups of a few varieties. For complex plantings, use simple layouts and avoid cluttering a small space with too much pattern.

Plants should be chosen and trained to reinforce design choices. For formal plots, boxwood, yew, ilex, and fast-growing privet thrive on clipping and make good hedges and topiary; neat fastigiate (narrow, upright-branching) trees like Irish yew, Italian cypress, American arborvitae, and Engelmann spruce form tall accents. Arching shrubs, spilling perennials, and waving grasses take naturally to meandering walks. As with grammar, once you understand the rules, you can break them with confidence: Plant beans in your parterre or make your cacti march in rows, for example. As the great English landscape designer Russell Page put it, "I like gardens with good bones and an affirmed underlying structure." The rest is up to you, and to nature.

PLAYING SQUARE

Since the dawn of history—and maybe even before—dividing land into square plots has been mankind's favorite for bringing order to the unruly character of plants. First we think square, then we find multiple ways to break up the basic figure. Each of the designs shown opposite could be a plan for anything from a condominium patio that's hemmed in by flagstones to an Elizabethan knot garden of herbs that's bounded by hedges of clipped boxwood, to a large-scale formal flower garden with miles of gravel paths.

CHARLES A PLATT His Place at CORNISH

A LINEAR ARRAY OF PATHS AND TERRACES (*left*) inspired by Italian Renaissance gardens, was laid out at the turn of the century by architect Charles A. Platt for his own home in New Hampshire. Functioning like outdoor rooms that extend the house, the entrance court (1), vegetable/cutting garden (2), flower gardens (3), porch (4), and tennis court (5) add up to a strong framework that has adapted gracefully to changes brought by three generations.

SPIRALING CIRCLES GIVE DASH AND LIVABILITY to landscape designer Diane Sjoholm and architect Ernest Schiefferstein's small sloped lot (*right*). A stone path (2) steps down from the sunny outdoor living room (1) to a shady glen (3) where a sculptural inlay squares the spiral.

A plan for the natural garden

Free-flowering and day-blooming, *Nymphaea*
'Patricia' is especially good for small pools but
also thrives in medium and large ones.

EVERY WOMAN KNOWS that the natural look takes some contriving to achieve, and every gardener who strives to make a garden look as if it happened all by itself soon learns the same thing: effortless beauty requires as much careful planning as does clipped and formal. You'd never know it in this naturalistic water-and-woodland corner of Alix and Joel Segal's four-acre property in East Hampton, Long Island, but nature's contribution was minimal—just a grudging, overgrown tangle of weeds, scrub oak, and pine trees in a slightly scooped-out depression of land. It was that scooped-out dent in the land that got designers Thomas Reinhardt and Mark Moscowitz (of his Wainscott, New York, firm, Landscape Design) thinking. And what they thought was *pond*. Or better yet, two ponds.

The Segals' house is sited so that its primary views overlook the gardens they have been creating, with the designers' help, since 1984, six years after the couple bought the house. They have a sweeping, sunny perennial border that beckons you from a brick terrace, and a dramatic pool garden that feels like a grotto: gardens out in the open, gardens that call to you at once. But there remained that tangled half-acre, the first thing you saw when you drove onto the property—an eyesore, too, from many windows in the house. It just took some plastic, a pump, and the right plantings to transform this mundane landscape into, well, a "natural" setting, one that invites both contemplation and a childlike delight in what nature is (and isn't) capable of providing on its own. "You're supposed to slow down as you approach," Joel Segal says. "You're supposed to be surprised, as if you were once again eight years old." And you do slow down, whether walking to it from the open garden, through the tunnels formed by tall ornamental grasses as they grow together, or approaching it more stealthily, through hosta-lined paths that wend their way to the water's edge.

To create the Segals' water feature, which starts out as a burbling stream by the driveway and eventually tumbles over two waterfalls before it comes to rest first in one pond, then in a second (and is then recirculated by pumps at either end, hidden by woodland plantings), the designers cleared and dug out the inferior soil to make way for the rich new soil they'd later mix from scratch

TO MAKE A GARDEN SEEM
NATURAL, BUILDING ON WHAT
NATURE HAS DONE ISN'T
NECESSARY; BUILDING AN
INFRASTRUCTURE IS. *This
tranquil, water lily–studded pond
began life as a scrubby, weedy, sandy
hollow in one corner of a garden. The
first step, bulldozing out the scrub,
produced space for two ponds but
tapped no springs to feed them. Once
a plastic liner to hold piped-in water,
a pumping system to recycle it, and
new soil to welcome plants were in
place, the creation of a pool-and-bog
garden could begin.*

215

the natural garden

(the poor, sandy soil, which also had marl and blue clay in it, was combined with such organic materials as cottonseed meal, peanut hulls, and composted manure). Cloth padding was laid into the now-deeper depression, which was then covered with a Geotex rubber lining; next, sand was spread on top of the lining, again for a "natural" look.

The designers extended the lining in many places well beyond the banks of the ponds, so that the amended soil could be artfully distributed on the newly planted shoreline, along with local driftwood and rocks hauled in from New Jersey and Pennsylvania.

From there, the real aesthetic decisions had to be made; ultimately, the ponds would only look as good—and as natural—as the plantings. "It was a matter of letting everything develop the way you want it to, and it wants to," says Alix Segal. "You can't force it." No, you can't force the natural look. But the Segals and their designers painstakingly evoked it with their choices of plants to grow in the ponds (such as water lilies and *Nymphoides cordata*), at water's edge (primula, Solomon's seal, rodgersia, aruncus), and along the surrounding woodland paths (ferns, dicentra, hostas, thalictrum). Even after

CHOOSING PLANTS THAT WILL LIKE THE HOME YOU'VE MADE FOR THEM— AND EACH OTHER—IS ESSENTIAL TO MAKING THE GARDEN LOOK AS IF IT HAD SIMPLY DONE WHAT CAME NATURALLY. It isn't only the water lilies and **Nymphoides cordata** *floating on the surface that give these pools their long-settled look. Even more important are the traditional denizens of the water's edge: the corydalis spilling over the waterside rocks; the cattails and variegated acorus thrusting up from the shallows* (**opposite**); *and the clumps of hostas and showy, summer-blooming* **Iris ensata** *massed on the shore* (**above**). *The plastic liner was carried back 10 feet from the edges of the pools in some places to undergird a broad and deep layer of new, rich soil. Now a seemingly indigenous succession of water-loving and woodland plants—aruncus, primulas, rodgersias, ligularias, joe-pye weed, Solomon's seal, thalictrum, and* **Lychnis chalcedonica**—*are thriving and spreading up into the woods that surround the pools, which have also been enriched with new plantings.*

installing drains that catch fallen leaves, the Segals and the designers sought out trees that wouldn't shed heavily and clog the ponds. When the sassafras trees died ("If one dies, they all die," says Joel), the skeletal trunks were kept in place for their sculptural effect—a collaboration between Mother Nature and Father Time.

Now this water-and-woodland garden feels inevitable, as if it has always existed. The paths give softly as you bounce along, the way the mossy floor of a virgin forest does. And a profusion of flowers tumbles over rocks and banks, in and out of the woods, in seeming abandon. This sleight of hand requires as much patient upkeep as the more obvious manicure of clipped topiaries and parterres. It's just that the spell would be broken if one drop of polish showed.

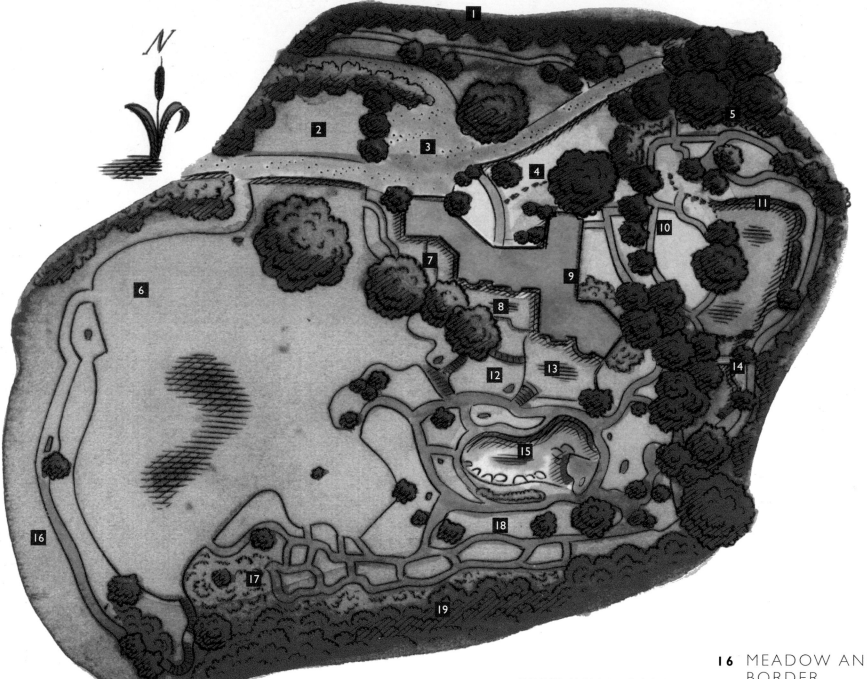

PLAN KEY

The irregular footprint of the house, the meandering route of the paths, and the undulating contours of ponds and swimming pool are echoed in sinuous perennial beds, bold clumps of trees, and sweeping meadows and woods.

1 SECRET GARDEN

2 LAWN AREA

3 DRIVEWAY

4 GROUND COVER AREA

5 BOG GARDEN

6 LAWN

7 ROCK GARDEN

8 PERENNIAL GARDEN

9 HOUSE

10 WOODLAND GARDEN

11 LARGE POND

12 PATH GARDEN

13 TERRACE

14 SMALL POND

15 SWIMMING POOL

16 MEADOW AND BORDER

17 LARGE PERENNIAL BORDER

18 PATH GARDEN

19 PRIVACY SCREEN OF TREES

IT IS CRUCIAL TO STUDY
WHAT NATURE ACTUALLY DOES
IN THE SITUATION YOU'RE
RE-CREATING. *Stonework in
particular can look very artificial
unless the stones are placed as they
would be in their original setting.
Plants soften edges, but they can't
disguise the awkwardness of rocks laid
at unnatural angles. To construct such
perfectly unconstructed-looking
cascades as those in the Segals' garden,
it helps to observe streams in the rocks'
home territory and see what the
patterns of fracture and erosion in
streambeds and waterfalls look like.*

DESIGNING A POND

It is easier than you might imagine to have a pond with all the trimmings, but think before you dive. To find out where a pond will look best, take stock of the lay of the land from every vantage point. Make sure that the surface of the water will reflect the most attractive features of your garden. You don't want to end up gazing at two garages, for example, whereas a stand of columbines, native azaleas, and red swamp maples would be doubly delightful mirrored in the pond. Beware of windswept sites, because many aquatic plants prefer still water. Partial shade, however, is not a problem. Lots of aquatic plants thrive in such conditions; but avoid picking a spot overhung by trees. Falling leaves clutter the surface of a pool, and as they decay, algae will proliferate.

Experiment with contours for a pond by laying a length of rope or hose on the ground (if you plan to line the cavity with a preformed fiberglass shell, the hole you dig must, of course, conform to its shape). Dig out the cavity to a depth of 2 to 3 feet; this will allow for enough water to accommodate plants and fish. To waterproof the bottom, use a flexible liner, such as sheets of PVC (polyvinyl chloride), 45-mil thick EPDM rubber, or clay-impregnated cloth. For a neatly architectural rim, use hardscaping materials like flagstones or bricks to cover the edge of the lining where it laps over the ground surrounding the pond; for more naturalistic banks, haul in large rocks or boulders. Avoid creating a bitsy "necklace" of small stones around the water.

Maintain a healthy ratio of plants and fish to water. About half the surface of a pond should be covered by water lilies, *Nymphaea*, and other floating plants. For every two square yards of surface, you'll need one medium-to-large water lily and two containers of plants. For every square yard of surface, a pond can usually support 9 inches' worth of fish. Install a pump with a mechanical or biological filter to process fish wastes and decomposing plants. A device capable of handling about 750 gallons per hour will keep a 100-square-foot pond clean. Mown turf grass shouldn't grow close to the pond's edge , since clippings will fall in and foul the water. When all is said and done, a do-it-yourself 2- to 3-foot-deep pond with 100 square feet of surface area will probably cost about $1,500 for materials, pump, plants, and fish. Hiring a contractor will add $3,000 to $4,500 to the bill.

THE PLANTS

Introducing oxygen to the water in a pond suppresses algal population explosions. You should, therefore, include some oxygenating specimens like *Elodea canadensis*, cambomba, or willow moss (these species also absorb harmful salts). Container growing is essential in tiny pools. Plants can be set at precisely the right depth, and tender ones can be brought inside over the winter.

THE FISH

Keep mosquito larvae down with goldfish such as golden orfe. They swim near the water's surface, so you'll see flashes of color as they cruise the pond. Japanese koi, on the other hand, are less spectacular, since they spend more time on the bottom, digging up the roots of water plants. Two dozen 4-inch-long fish can live comfortably in a 100-square-foot pond. A small, immersible heater will prevent winter freeze-up.

A plan for combining many gardens in one

NEW YORK CITY'S CENTRAL PARK is, by any stretch of the imagination, a tough act to follow—but follow it Betsy Barlow Rogers did, right in her own backyard. She also learned from it, expanded upon it, and reached beyond it. But she definitely brought her work home with her and, for years, Rogers's work was Central Park.

Though many gardeners begin with a crisp two- or five-year plan, Rogers, by her own admission, didn't have a master plan at all. She bought her house—an eastern Long Island shingled farmhouse with a vegetable garden—in 1965 and raised her two children, some marigolds, and a few vegetables early on, all the while working on a book about Central Park's designer, Frederick Law Olmsted. Later, she became both the Park Administrator and president of the Central Park Conservancy, the private organization that took on the daunting task of reviving the park and succeeded. Today, this not-for-profit citizens' group raises two-thirds of the park's budget. Rogers herself oversaw the raising of $150 million for Central Park's recent renovation. Like a sleeping princess awakened in a fairy tale, the park began to flourish. So did Rogers's sense of what she wanted in her garden.

She started a cottage garden, inspired by a trip to England in 1974, before she actually tackled the park; if a farmhouse could ask for a garden, this enchanted but straightforward space is surely the garden it would ask for. "I came back with ideas about foliage and floral color, plant shapes and combinations, as well as a new love of old roses," she says. Tucked close to the house as if for shelter and incorporating a small, quirky shed, this enclosed, picket-fenced area is where she planted tumbling-over flower beds after laying bricks to create pathways and define beds. Later, Lynden Miller, who was working on restoring the park's Conservatory Garden, advised Rogers on what would enhance her own garden's formal structure. Rogers remembers, "Lynden told me about 'careless rapture'— how great it is to have things flopping over and spilling, as long as they're spilling against something." Now Rogers has perennials and annuals spilling against angular,

At the oak-shaded entrance to a 1906 Long Island farmhouse, 'Bright Eyes' phlox leans over a split-rail fence.

AN ENCLOSED, GEOMETRIC GARDEN EXTENDS A HOUSE AND HELPS ANCHOR IT IN THE LANDSCAPE. *Architectural in layout but clothed in plants, such garden rooms provide a transition to less obviously structured parts of a garden, and may be intended for outdoor living or purely for visual pleasure. This cottage garden's white picket fence and box-edged beds—shown filled with blue ageratum—resonate perfectly with the turn-of-the-century farmhouse, as does the yearly change of colorful annuals in the stone urn, here planted with Helichrysum petiolare.*

224

TO NINETEENTH-CENTURY GARDEN MAKERS, RUSTIC ARBORS, BRIDGES, SEATS, AND SUMMERHOUSES OF UNPEELED LOGS AND TWIGS WERE NECESSARY AND PROPER FURNISHINGS FOR PICTURESQUE LANDSCAPES. *Benches built into Rogers's wisteria-hung arbor (above) designed by David Robinson, offer a place to sit and enjoy cool shade on a hot summer day. Her natural-seeming woods and rustic structures were carefully sited and planted just like the woodland rambles that Frederick Law Olmsted created in Central Park, and like the gnarly arbors (left) that his collaborator, Calvert Vaux, created there. Betsy Barlow Rogers, former Administrator of Central Park, standing near a park bench (above right), selected the river stones for her arbor's path and collected the ferns that feather its edges.*

clipped boxwoods, against the old shed, the picket fence, and bricks, as well as out of a centerpiece urn.

Rogers also used structure to give a sense of focus to the front yard. Where originally visitors forged their own trail to enter the house, now there are welcoming flagstone paths to lead the way, and the entry has been planted to suggest the scale of the cottage garden to come. But there's more. A gate leading through the picket fence on one side of the house opens onto a landscape so utterly different in sensibility that you want occasionally to run back to touch the pickets, as if they were home base, before going off to explore some more. Rogers, with a little help from her Central Park designer friends, has managed to create both mystery and majesty in a space neither mysterious nor majestic. Behind the clean lines of the house and the geometric precision of the cottage garden, Rogers's property wanders off; for years, her back lawn ended in a scrubby area thick with catbrier where she had always dreamed of making a woodland garden, perhaps with a pond. When Rogers met the late landscape architect Bruce Kelly in the mid-1980s, she began to realize her sylvan fantasy. "Bruce taught me about ground plane lines. I began to think about where the edges were, how to lead your eye. Paths are so important. I began to understand that the garden is a journey."

If the home base of the cottage garden is all about tidy symmetry, the journey starts as you emerge from it onto a back lawn edged

in boldly drawn curves. The first woodland screen you see—hemlocks, rhododendrons, some deciduous flowering shrubs—might be the end of the garden, but you know it's not, because the curving path that takes you there promises to lead you somewhere new. Sure enough, it widens into a clearing, with another path to guide you to a pond, where a bridge urges you to stop, listen to the water, and then move on to explore a forest of oaks and more hemlock. The farther back you go, the wilder it feels.

After Betsy Barlow married Ted Rogers, he, along with Bruce Kelly and David Robinson—the latter was restoring the rustic structures (the arbors and pergola) in Central Park—encouraged her to keep conquering each frontier of the garden and sculpting more of the land. Sweeps of lawn now end in woodland, it's true, but the curves are so fastidiously edged it's clear that nature has been reined in. Between lawns and woodland, the transition is firmly yet softly defined by masses of ground covers: ferns, aegopodium, bronze ajuga. Even the paths change mood—from tidy bricks to river stone to pine needles that muffle sound as the woods deepen.

As a bored preteen, Rogers's son, David, once cut an exploratory tunnel through the catbrier—and there discovered the perfect site for a pond. The body of water that Rogers asked Kelly and his partner, David Varnell, to design intentionally resembles the glaciated ponds, called kettleholes, that dot the Long Island landscape. The rustic bridge that Robinson built over it has railings of cedar, pressure-treated pine supports, and decking of a sustainably harvested South American wood, *Tabebuia* spp. Robinson created a rustic cedar bench for the spot where you first hear moving water, as well as a romantic black-locust arbor.

Another key decision Rogers made was surely influenced by her work in Central Park, that most public of spaces. In her corner of Long Island, she decided, "Good fences wouldn't necessarily make good neighbors," so she asked the neighbors whether she could extend her sight lines and curves onto their properties. Now you can't quite tell where the garden begins and ends, much to the neighbors' delight. Indeed, a neighbor's daughter asked to get married in what she called the glen—and the glen is what the middle clearing has been called ever since. However personal and private Rogers's own garden may be, her impulse is perhaps the same one that drew her to Central Park: a calling to bring nature to people and people to nature. Her grander muse, Central Park, has served her well here at home.

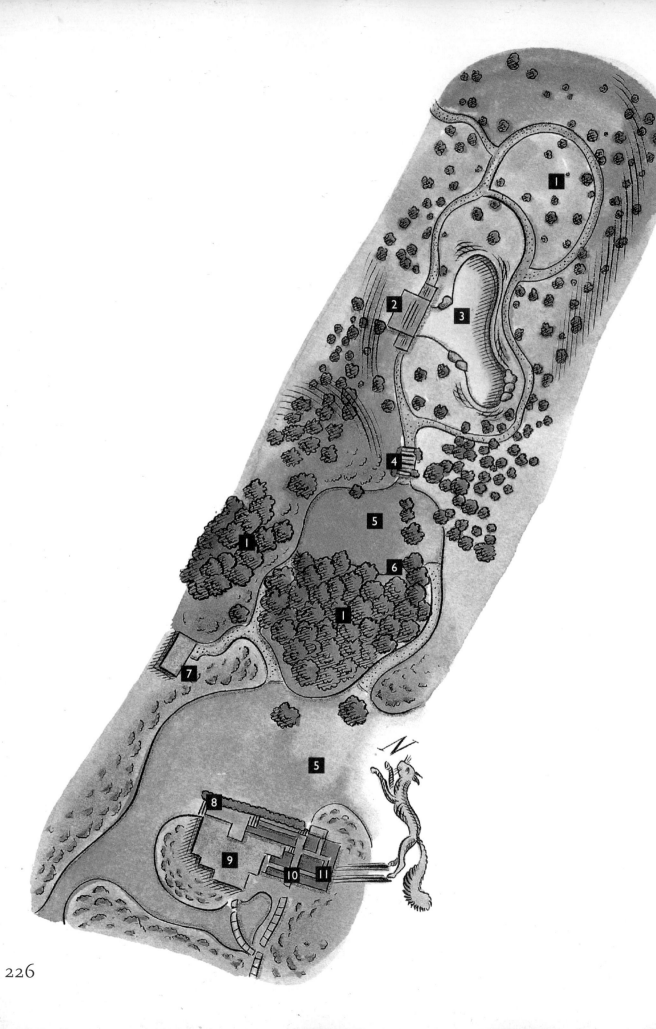

PLAN KEY

In the great public parks that Frederick Law Olmsted masterminded in the nineteenth century, he strategically mapped out carriage roads and pedestrian paths to link landscapes with very different functions into one harmonious sequence of journeys and destinations. Though privately owned, domestic in scale, and geared to late-twentieth-century living, this garden-of-many-parts honors Olmsted's ideals.

1 WOODLAND

2 BRIDGE

3 POND

4 RUSTIC ARBOR

5 LAWN

6 RUSTIC BENCH

7 SHED

8 DECK

9 HOUSE

10 ROSE ARBOR

11 COTTAGE GARDEN

CAREFULLY MODULATED
CONTRASTS BETWEEN SHADY
WOODS AND SUNNY CLEARINGS
ADD MYSTERY AND MOVEMENT TO
A LANDSCAPE. *Beds laid out in curves*
help to direct eye and foot. Less structured
than the cottage garden, a lawn to the
southeast of the house represents another
stage in the picturesque garden's tradi-
tional outward progression from order to
wildness at the edge of the property.

A NECKLACE OF PATHS LINKS SPACES OF VARIED MOODS; ARCHES AND ARBORS FRAME VISTAS AND TEMPT THE VISITOR TO ENTER THEM. An arbor bewigged in 'New Dawn' roses (above) crowns the gate into the cottage garden. A matching archway at the far side announces that more lies beyond. **Opposite:** *The same rose arbor beckons from the front yard. To reach it, you follow stepping stones brushed by lamium, spirea, astilbe, and oakleaf hydrangea.*

DESIGNING AN ARBOR

Formal or rustic, an arbor is a graceful way to let the visitor know where to go and how to get there. Formal arbors paraphrase classic architectural forms: an arch, a portal, perhaps a column twined with roses. Landscape designer David Varnell has used a variety of types of wood for his precisely cut, shaped, and fitted arbors. His decision depends on whether they are to be painted or stained, as is the case with white pine, or, allowed to weather, as redwood is. White isn't the only paint choice—blue, gray, brown, and black blend with the surroundings. Use green with care: it can clash with natural shades of this color (a dark green paint or stain, with black mixed in, is best if you want to use this hue).

"Looking natural is the point of rustic construction," says David Robinson, the man responsible for much of the restored rustic architecture in New York's Central Park. For an arbor that works well in a woodsy garden or forms a transition between wild and formal areas, he studies the sizes, shapes, and irregularities of cut tree trunks and branches, then carefully selects and joins them, taking his cues from nature. "I observe trees," Robinson explains. "They are gracefully proportioned naturally."

Any arbor must be anchored with a foundation that extends below the frost line. The piers you sink into the ground can be masonry, concrete, or pressure-treated wood. Don't use pressure-treated wood for the structure, though: it takes paint poorly and is hard to nail or screw. Whatever you use, it should be the best you can afford. In some climates, metals work better than wood; landscape architect Michael Van Valkenburgh used stainless steel for an arbor at the Walker Art Center in Minneapolis. And if the arbor has to support a vigorous grower like wisteria, it must be sturdier than one that just gives a lift to a moonflower vine. If you want to do joinery, be sure to use top-quality paint, and stainless-steel screws. But proportions here are crucial, and to get them right you often have to make the arbor larger than what may be structurally necessary. As a rule of thumb, use heavier timbers and make the structure taller and wider than you first thought necessary. Less experienced carpenters, however, may want to use simple butted connections.

THE FORMAL ARBOR at the entrance to Betsy Barlow Rogers's cottage garden (*below*) is a classic arch smothered in 'New Dawn' roses. White paint echoes the house's trim and the garden's picket fence.

THE RUSTIC ARBOR in the Rogers garden (*right*) took "a well-stocked woodpile, a good eye, the ability to cut simple joints, and lots of experimental fitting," says its creator, David Robinson. He modified his design along the way to incorporate pieces that suggest arches and bays.

A plan for a small-scale container garden

WITH A TINY PLOT, you make a diminutive garden in keeping with the scale. Right? Well, that's the conventional wisdom, but designer Bill Goldsmith, decidedly *un*conventional, has taken exactly the opposite tack in his exquisite, highly personal, and definitely tiny garden. The message he conveys is this: When the scale is small, dare to think big. Create outdoor rooms and furnish every inch of them. Fill up the space with beds of plants along the perimeters and plants everywhere else, too, in dozens of imaginatively chosen pots. In other words, bring the richness and complexity of a larger landscape into this little space. Add some ornamental outdoor collectibles (vintage watering cans, a world-class hose-nozzle collection) and a sculptural obelisk to serve as a focal point. Have only furniture that's designed to be lived in, get weatherbeaten, then lived in some more, and you'll have a garden that's crammed with personality, with plenty of room for spirit and flair.

Cheek by jowl with cottages on either side, Goldsmith's property has the flow of a railroad apartment. Umbrella-shaded garden room in front, then the cottage, and another umbrella-shaded garden room in back, leading to a little wooden dock set in a man-made lagoon that flows in from San Francisco Bay. The nine-foot-high garden walls were already in place when Goldsmith, who paints botanical watercolors, designs fabric, wallpaper, and furniture, and who has also designed porce-

Layers of whimsy and ornament abound in Goldsmith's chock-full garden. Here, weathered finials are bedecked with beads.

TERRACES, DECKS, PORCHES, AND PATIOS ARE PRIME LOCATIONS FOR GARDENS PLANTED IN POTS AND BOXES. Your outdoor area may have or need a hard surface, as Bill Goldsmith's does (right), but that doesn't mean you can't grow plants. Container-based, they can star as structure—suggesting walls or framing a view—and as living decoration thereby turning once hard-edged spaces into inviting open-air rooms.

lain, began his garden three years ago by tearing out everything except the few existing trees, including a magnolia and a pollarded plum. In place, too, was cement-aggregate decking, which "gets all crookedy and a bit hard to deal with," with room for narrow flower beds surrounding it. Then, he says, "I started in one corner, moved to another, and just kept rearranging all my stuff."

Surely one can rearrange stuff with more confidence—and success—if one is a gifted designer to begin with, but there are ideas and lessons here for anyone to adapt. Even if the display is movable, for example, the classic form of boxwoods in ornate pots gives a defining structure to Goldsmith's garden, and seems solid and weighted in contrast to the whimsical flourishes set or growing all around. The obelisk (made, like the furniture, in Java from teak) is another formal structural element, and provides an emphatic verticality, drawing the eye upward from the small tract and beyond it to the broad lagoon. The

Ivy-hung trellis and datura growing in a garbage can flank the cabinet that holds Goldsmith's world-class collection of hose nozzles.

furniture Goldsmith designed has an unmistakably indoor-outdoor feel—a wooden bench whose tufted seats are carved, a stool, its wooden "webbing" carved in curves to look like woven rushes, and a graceful teak chair with cushions slipcovered in a Goldsmith print fabric that replicates his array of watering cans—smoothing the transition from house to garden.

Goldsmith also has a wonderful eye (and appetite) for choosing plants that do amusing things: the occasional topiary clipped like a corkscrew, English pottery "stumps" filled with agaves and succulents next to pots of horsetails growing straight up (chosen, he says, "because they were so weird"), everyday zinnias, exotic-looking daturas, and more succulents juxtaposed with frilly flowers that seem to float. There's coleus, more somber, here and there, and basil, sage, and morning glory in pots. "The garden relaxes me after working," Goldsmith explains, "and then I feel like working again." Like a tiny horticultural studio writ large, Bill Goldsmith's garden is a repository of ideas, memories—and ever more "stuff" to rearrange.

THERE ARE HARDLY ANY LIMITS TO THE MOODS AND DECORATIVE STYLES CONTAINER GARDENS CAN EXPRESS. Classic or romantic, spare or stuffed like a Victorian parlor, container gardens are also a snap to rearrange. Trying different effects with the happily cohabiting flowers, foliage, and man-made forms on this collector's terrace is just a matter of moving pots, though shifting the heavy ones may require a dolly.

235

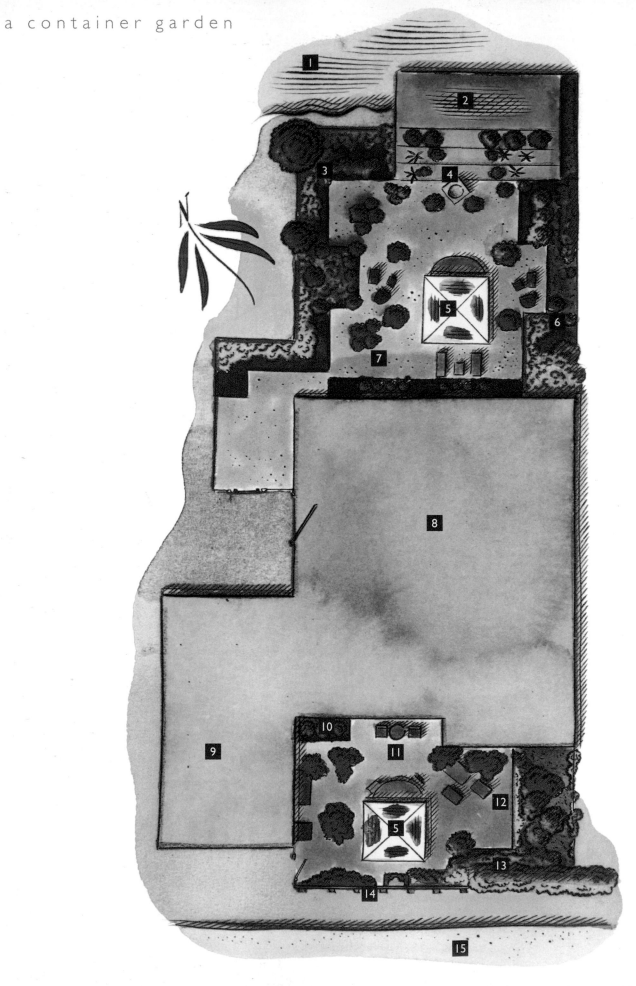

PLAN KEY

Except for a few fixed elements that mark the boundaries of the two outdoor rooms—house, garage, dock, and fences—the plan of this garden is constantly in flux. The two umbrella-topped dining tables tend to remain in place as the central focus of each room, but the rest of the furnishings, including the containers that hold most of the plants, are a movable feast for the eye.

1 LAGOON

2 DOCK

3 ROSES

4 OBELISK

5 DINING TABLE

6 RAISED BED

7 LAGOON GARDEN

8 HOUSE

9 GARAGE

10 HYDRANGEAS

11 KITCHEN GARDEN

12 HERBS

13 CAMELLIAS

14 ESPALIERED ASIAN PEAR TREE

15 STREET

SMALL SPACES WORK BEST WHEN THEIR BASIC PLANS ARE
SIMPLE FRAMEWORKS THAT CAN BE RICHLY DETAILED. *Bill
Goldsmith's garden comprises two tiny enclosures at either end of his house,
which fills the entire width of a narrow lot. The larger area faces northeast
and looks out on a lagoon leading into San Francisco Bay; the smaller faces
south and has no view. Both have been given a similar treatment. Each has as
its focus a central umbrella-shaded table with four chairs, and the waterfront
area has room as well for a tub chair and tea table.*

*All of these pieces plus some of the ornaments were designed by Goldsmith
and are from his collection for Sutherland. At this point simplicity ends.
Plant-filled containers pile up around the perimeter and seem to flow into
any available space. The flowerpot decorated with ceramic fragments perched
on the table next to Nigel the cat (above) was designed by Goldsmith as
was the teakwood version of a classical planter (right). The planting in and
around it are a key to the garden's successful harmonizing of its
eclectic mix of plants and containers. They are everywhere grouped into
miniature gardens. In this case the pink and white of the ornamental sage
and nicotiana in the box are complemented by the encircling pots of dianthus,
pale green zinnias, and basil. For drama, who could resist the leaves of
the zonal pelargonium (above right)? Certainly not a designer of fabrics,
another of Goldsmith's specialties.*

DESIGNING WITH POTS

Ashapely, generously proportioned container can give as much style to a garden as the plants you put in it, and while small plants are just starting out, your pot can dominate the scene. If, when you're shopping, one shape stands out from the crowd, consider buying several of it. Matched containers unify a terrace, dignify an entrance, or herald a path or a vista.

Drainage is the key to a healthy container plant. If there isn't a hole in the bottom of a planter, you will have to drill one or have it drilled by the purveyor. Lay shards of broken terra-cotta pots over the hole to keep soil in while allowing water to run through. Even small trees and shrubs need a soil depth of no more than 12 inches for healthy root growth. Conserve soil in deeper containers by filling them below the 12-inch depth with styrofoam packing peanuts or gravel (the weight of gravel keeps tall containers from tipping over in strong winds).

Bagged potting soil is too fine to absorb water well. A better planting medium is a mix of 3 parts moist peat to 1 part weed-free topsoil. Fill containers up to 1 inch below the rim, then scratch in time-release fertilizer or, for plants that need rich soil, add commercial composted cow manure to the soil mix. As for the plants you choose, remember that appealing foliage textures; vivid colors like purple, golden, and gray, or variegated hues; and sculptural form are as important as heavy flowering. Use tall plants to anchor the center of the pot; let spreaders drape over the edge. If newly purchased plants are blooming heavily, clip off flowers and buds to encourage shoot and root growth. Water right after planting to settle the soil. Thereafter, check soil moisture regularly and water often, probably at least once a week, because potted plants dry out more quickly than those set in the earth.

If winter temperatures in your area typically drop below freezing, empty all containers in the fall. If you do not take potted annuals, or cuttings, indoors, compost them; plant shrubs and perennials in the ground. Overwinter containers indoors or turn them upside down or cover them tightly to keep out water, which will cause cracking as it freezes and expands.

LAYER SPRING BULBS

For the earliest possible container-plant color, fill pots thickly with bulbs in the fall. The diagram (1) shows planting depths. Deeper bulbs will grow up through shallower ones. Store the pots at about 35°F, and put them outdoors in spring.

MIX HEIGHTS

A selection of small pots, as in (3), can create a big impression. Similar glazes and jarlike forms unify a collection of short-to-tall containers.

TRY VARIOUS MATERIALS

Options include glazed and unglazed terra-cotta, concrete, stoneware, aluminum, wood, fiberglass, plastic, and cast iron, like the urn in (2). Plants in glazed containers and plastic pots need less frequent watering than those in concrete or terra-cotta.

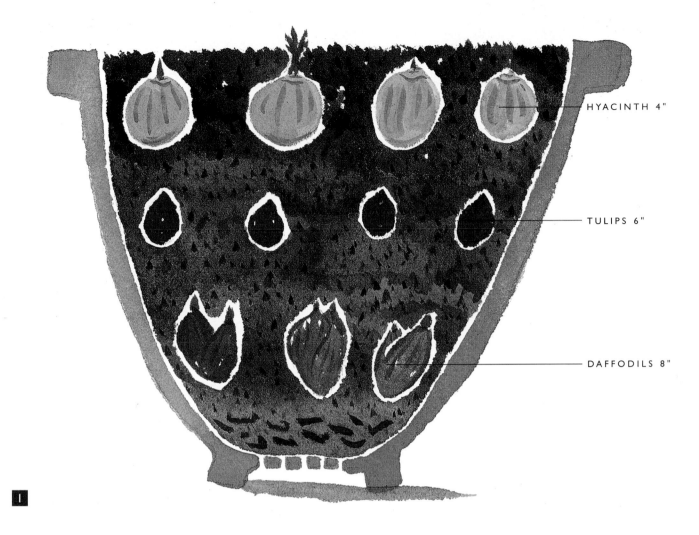

HYACINTH 4"

TULIPS 6"

DAFFODILS 8"

1

2

3

A plan for the shade garden

LIKE FAIRY TALES with happy endings, many gardeners' true stories echo the same theme: The gardener buys a pathetic house with problematic grounds and, over time and against great odds, fixes up the house and makes the garden of his dreams. Sometimes the vision is there from the beginning; more often it evolves as the dream settles into the land.

These were the challenges facing Michael Bates: an unprepossessing farmhouse that seemed oddly unconnected to the five acres of land around it, a jumble of chain-link gates and fences, asphalt, and Bermuda grass that wouldn't budge—not the most welcome sight to a man with a garden in mind. True, the land was situated 1,100 feet up Sonoma Mountain, an hour's drive north of San Francisco, and had an unusual ecosystem that could nourish an astounding variety of plants— apples and oranges in the same orchard, for instance. But it was also true that the land closest to the house, pleasingly shaped like a cradle, was shaded by oak, madrone, and 80-foot California bay trees, *Umbellularia californica*. In keeping with the myth, however, he and his wife, Helen, ultimately realized that they'd never find the place of their dreams, and in 1982 they decided to create it here. It took many renovations and many versions of their garden to get there.

Bates, who had gardened off and on since childhood, started out by disappearing into the landscape. "As a transplanted Englishman, I wanted to translate my visions and memories, so that first rainy February, I began to plant rhododendrons everywhere under the oaks. Lo and behold, by the first week in April: no more rain, and everything started to die. I ran around like a lunatic with a hose. It was a quick learning curve. If you want to grow things up here that need water, you need an irrigation system." And deer fencing, and rich new soil to cover the rock- and root-bound terrain, and pruning equipment to seduce carefully selected shafts of light. Two steps forward, one step back.

The rhododendrons-under-the-oaks scheme came directly from Bates's recollection of the English woods he'd explored as a child, where understories of wild shrubs and flowers flourished beneath the high leafy canopies of trees. His mem-

MATTE, GLOSSY, FINE, BOLD, LACY, VELVETY—LEAVES IN ALL THEIR TONES OF GREEN ARE THE SHADE GARDENER'S BASIC PALETTE. Shade-loving flowers do exist, even green ones like **Helleborus orientalis**, *which blends right in with majestic blue* **Hosta fortunei** *'Hyacinthina', variegated* **H. sieboldii**, *ornamental grass, and navelwort on the forest floor. Red columbines play a more usual flower part as bright but fleeting grace notes in this foliage ensemble.*

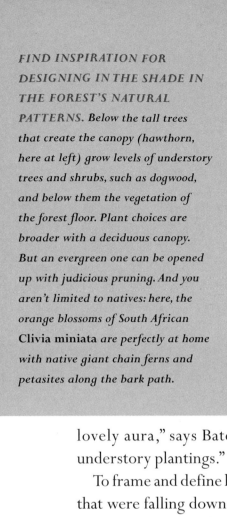

ories also nurtured dreams of the gardens that would emerge from his American woodlands: sunny open borders, swags of roses, a magical wild garden where nature would have the final say, a vegetable garden, and an orchard (which today yields plenty of apples for hard cider, along with oranges, peaches, plums, and apricots).

Where most of us would perhaps (sensibly) give up before we even started (madly) cultivating root-bound soil under 80-foot bay trees, Bates was undeterred. "Shade," he says, "isn't a problem, and what it actually gives you is greater flexibility in styles." He points out the ways in which gardeners take sunny spaces and then set about casting shade, deliberately or not, with arbors, pergolas, and other structures that are heavy with plants growing over them; and there will always be levels of higher-growing plants blocking the light from shorter companions. The gardener will forever be chasing sun around the garden. "Our bay trees provide dappled sunlight throughout the day, which creates a lovely aura," says Bates. "First, you have to study the light. Only then can you work on the understory plantings."

To frame and define his shade garden, Bates put in rustic fencing and rebuilt stone retaining walls that were falling down all over the property. Next, he filled in terraces behind the walls, heaping each level with two feet of new soil he mixed by combining topsoil with organic matter. He viewed the trees as architectural features, the living columns and vaulted ceilings of natural arbors and rooms, planting the understories along a network of paths. "I've tried to establish three or even more levels," he says, "and now we have dogwoods and snowbell trees [*Styrax*], small trees that 'embower' you in an understory 15 or 20 feet high." As each level of the garden grew at its own pace, he'd plant yet another understory beneath it, weaving on the woodland floor a tapestry as intricately patterned as a Persian carpet.

The woodland space comprises barely half an acre but feels much larger, since the only way to view it is along the meandering paths. Stone here, different grades of bark there, the paths set off the varied plantings and provide natural transitions from glade to glade. It's a forest you can lose yourself in, and yet still easily find your way back out, to the reassuring openness of the sunnier, tamer gardens around the house. "I prefer that the transition happen in a natural way," says Bates, "not with abrupt changes." So you blink when you come out of the woods and into the sun, and the texture of the pathway changes, too, to tell you you're in a new place.

"The tall trees gave immediate structure, a framework to design the garden around," Bates explains, "and I'm elaborating on that, making the forest feel like a garden and heightening the sense of enclosure." Painstakingly layered with color and texture, his enchanted understories make the available light seem like just enough. Wondrously, it is.

Perennial *Geranium maderense*, a vigorous self-seeder, lights up the ground under magnolias and deutzias.

CONSIDER PLANTS THAT NATURALLY THRIVE AT THE FOREST EDGE FOR SUNNY SPOTS IN A SHADY GARDEN. *They tend to find conditions to their liking and visibly smooth the transition between woods and lawn.* Above: *white foxgloves join forces with* Phlomis fruiticosa, Euphorbia x martinii, *'Bowles Golden' sedge, golden oregano, and white calla lilies to brighten a shrub-bordered path and clearing.*

the shade garden

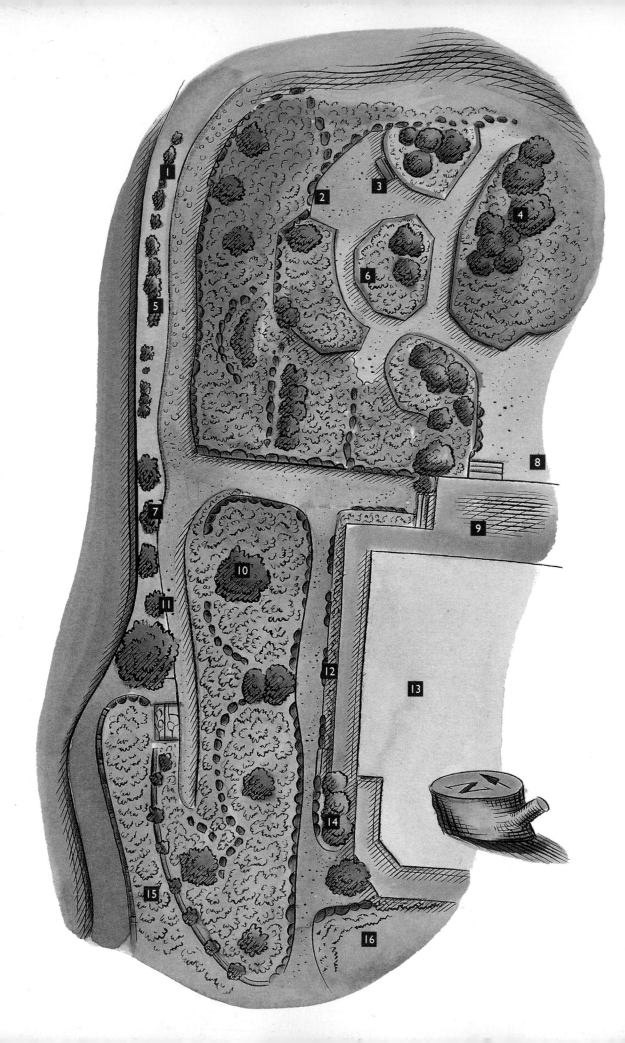

PLAN KEY

Paths wind away from the
sunny clearing around the house,
offering intriguing glimpses
into the garden's shady depths.
The circuitous routes combine
with meandering, multilevel
terraces and dense plantings to
make the property seem
far more extensive than it is.

1 BLACKBERRIES

2 ROCKS

3 BENCH

4 REDWOODS

5 VALERIAN

6 NATIVE ORCHIDS

7 CAMELLIA

8 VIOLETS, EUPHORBIA,
AND PRIMROSES

9 REDWOOD DECK

10 *CORNUS FLORIDA*
'CLOUD NINE'

11 AZALEA

12 STREAM

13 HOUSE

14 HYDRANGEAS

15 ROCK ROSES

16 LAWN AND
PERENNIAL BORDER

Carefully tended
and watered,
Rhododendrum x
loderi 'King George'
proves that it can
flourish in a less-
than-ideal climate.

DESIGNING FOR THE SHADE

Shady sites are a boon to gardeners. Shade envelops a space, sheltering plant matter and people alike from wind and hot sun. For plant lovers, it affords the opportunity to grow a vast number of beautiful woodland species that may not thrive in full sun. The main challenge for those designing for dark locations is that the color palette tends to be dominated by green, so unless you choose plants and hardscaping carefully, a shade garden may be needlessly monotonous and perhaps even gloomy.

Even the darkest part of such a site—ground level—can be made to look as though it is illuminated. As if by magic, low-growing plants with pale foliage seem to generate light. In fact, they are reflecting it. Fortunately, there are many plants that fall into this category and thereby serve as focal points for a woodland glade. Anything under two feet tall is effective in lighting up the forest floor. Many ground covers and garden perennials have pale green-to-chartreuse leaves; a smaller number have blue-green-to-gray foliage or variegated leaves—greenery that is striped or splashed with yellow or white. Hostas, which have handsome leaves in all these categories, are a staple for shade-garden design.

In addition, you can consider including patches of low-growing evergreen plants—such as hellebore, vinca, leucothoe, moss—to bring spots of color to the winter landscape when the shade garden, deprived of its deciduous canopy, suddenly becomes sunny for a few months.

There are various types of shade and degrees of darkness, and it's important to determine which kind you have before you begin to plant. Many woodland plants flower best in partial shade, that is, with three to six hours of sunlight each day. Dappled shade, where patches of sunlight show through the canopy of trees and pass briefly over the vegetation on the ground, is ideal.

Full, deep shade, where the green matter at ground level receives less than two hours of sun a day, is good only for true woodland plants. In most cases, deep shade is dry and infertile, because the tree roots compete for every ounce of water and nutrients. The soil in such areas needs to be amended with compost, leaf mold, or other organic material to increase both nutrients and moisture retention. If large trees in the area cast too many deep shadows, hire a professional tree service to thin the canopy and prune or remove lower limbs.

THE LAYERED LOOK

When designing under the canopy of large trees, follow nature's model, as illustrated at right (1), and arrange the understory plants in layers. Small trees will thrive beneath the majestic giants. Lower down, mix flowering forest shrubs with perennials. Pull the picture together at ground level with creepers and spring bulbs.

HIGH SHADE

When the canopy is raised and tall trees are widely spaced, as in Winterthur's Azalea Woods (2), there is ample light for bloom at ground level. Here, under a canopy of tulip poplars, white-flowered dogwood branches appear to hover behind Kurume azaleas. Bluebells and phlox carpet the forest floor.

DAPPLED SHADE

In Winterthur's Glade Garden (3), azaleas and yellow flag iris catch intermittent rays of sun.

A plan for the courtyard

IF YOU WERE LIVING in Europe or America a century ago and wanted to create a stylish, private garden, you'd almost certainly have incorporated statues and fountains inspired by classical motifs. Fast-forward to this century, this decade, and the Pacific Palisades, California, home of Charles Eglee and his wife, Ninkey Dalton. The desire for privacy is as strong as ever, but the artifacts that make it stylish come from sources closer to home. It's long been a principle of interior design to bring the outdoors in, to have glimpses of the garden from every room in the house. What Eglee and Dalton have done is to select their favorite indoor design elements and bring them outdoors, incorporating them into garden living rooms. If nature is the purest form of design, as both Dalton and Eglee believe, added ornament can set it off spectacularly.

This is a one-thing-led-to-another garden, on a tiny lot, 50 by 125 feet, much of it taken up by the house. The landscaping started with a hedge planted all around the property for privacy. Eglee, a writer-producer for film and television, chose eugenia because it grows fast. The hedge quickly walled off the front, which was already dominated by a huge, old cedar tree. The cedar seemed to define the whole garden and give it a mysterious aura. "At that point, our decisions were so dictated by practicality," Eglee says, "that aesthetics were almost secondary."

Well, yes and no. Dalton, a film and television production designer, had always dreamed, in her native Toronto, of having a swimming pool and a lemon tree from which she could pick her own lemons. She and Eglee planted the lemon tree, then turned to a friend, landscape architect Rob Steiner, to help them translate the pool dream into their real-life backyard, a space with a scrappy lawn way too small for a pool. The couple had already decided to make the backyard even smaller by building a wall that would divide it into two rooms. Steiner's solution was to make a courtyard with a koi pond outside the family room, and an herb patch ("our whatnot garden," Eglee calls it) way at the back, in what had been an overgrown vegetable garden. As the ornamental centerpiece for the pond, Eglee selected not classical sculpture from the distant past, but the "definitive piece" from his extensive collection of vintage Southern California–made Bauer pottery; gradually, more and more objects—like the chic 1950s concrete mannequin who eyes the front yard—began to adorn the garden.

These rooms continued to evolve. A garage that had to be torn down was rebuilt as a taller

EVEN A SMALL YARD, WALLED OR HEDGED FOR PRIVACY, CAN OFFER SURPRISING NEW LIVING SPACE. *Canny planning created two outdoor rooms, each about the size of a large living room, each with a water feature, on this little Los Angeles lot. Modern versions of traditional Mediterranean walled courtyards combine fresh-air pleasures like murmuring fountains and scented flowers with durable surfaces for playing or just standing and talking, comfortable seating, and intriguing decorative objects like Bauer pottery oil jars and Japanese glass fishing floats.*

251

structure, providing a perfect garden wall, which Dalton and Eglee had painted a glorious terra-cotta red. The walled room, which gets morning sun (and guests in the evening—this is where the family entertains) seems to glow in the golden light, as do the koi, the Bauer oil jar, the gravel-encircled pond, and the luxuriant plants. Another indoors-to-outdoors touch is a meditative painting on one of the garden walls, next to a door that leads to a wine cellar in the garage. Years before, the artist Nancy Kintisch, a friend, had painted the four-by-eight-foot canvas for Eglee and Dalton, but they never had a wall big enough to display it—until that garden wall. With the artist's permission, Eglee had the painting vinylized, and now it looks as if it had been painted just for this spot. Dalton designed the furniture for the garden, and Kintisch made a tile mosaic for the tabletop and decorative tile inlays for the cement and brick driveway.

Enjoying the view from the front steps: Charles Eglee, Ninkey Dalton, their daughter Eli Eglee, dalmatian Bongo, and (*front row right*), landscape architect Rob Steiner.

Only when the hedge had grown in around the front courtyard, Eglee says, did he begin to understand how a garden can be architectural, how it becomes a room. His early attempts at an English perennial border inside the hedge had never looked quite right against this Spanish-style house in California, so when oak root fungus killed the monumental cedar, he and Dalton, along with Steiner and his new partner, garden designer Jay Griffith, rethought this front room, transforming it from English border to Mission-style courtyard with a fountain. The couple had longed to hear water from the house, and now they do; the fountain (thanks to a pump, see Lesson Plan: Designing a Fountain, page 256) circulates through another Bauer pottery jar, linking the the front yard fountain to the backyard koi pool. Where foxgloves, columbine, and delphiniums once struggled in the heat, palms and more regionally suitable Mediterranean plants now thrive. As do New Zealand flax, *Phormium*, and nasturtium, which impart both hard edges and softness.

PLANTS OF MANY KINDS GIVE A SMALL SPACE GREATER EYE-APPEAL. Framed by the fragrant bells of **Brugmansia versicolor,** *the view from the front door takes in a richly planted corner.* **Solanum jasminoides** *tumbles over the eugenia hedge; in front of it, azaleas and camellias are punctuated by clumps of spiky phormium. At ground level, nasturtiums and* **Senecio mandraliscae** *flank the eye-catcher, a cast-concrete 1950s mannequin.*

The same painstaking precision with which many of us arrange and rearrange a coffee table, or an entire living room, is in evidence everywhere in this garden: the size, scale, and placement of the high-color Bauer pots; the siting of fountain and pool; the pragmatic design of furniture, and a floor plan that works; the harmony of the materials used for the floors and walls with the California "ceiling" above; and not least, the selection and care of the lush plants. Call it exterior decoration.

253

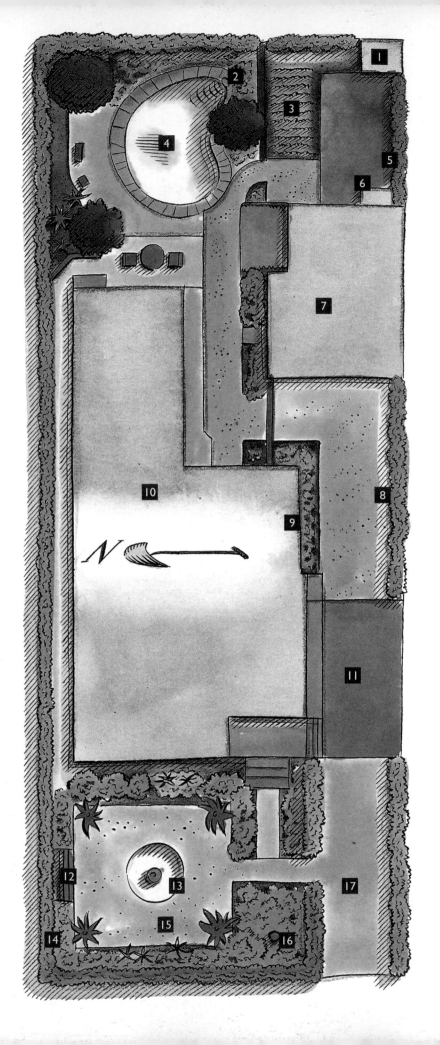

PLAN KEY

Given the tight fit of house, garage, and driveway on this 50-by-125-foot lot, the owners might well have resigned themselves to a vacant front lawn exposed to the street, and a backyard patio, and more lawn, where all outdoor living really takes place. Instead, ingenious dovetailing of hedges and garden walls turns every square inch, front and back, into welcoming, well-furnished courtyards.

1   POTTING SHED

2   BAUER OIL JAR FOUNTAIN

3   VEGETABLE BED

4   POOL

5   STEEL WALL PLANTER

6   GARDEN TOOLSHED

7   GARAGE

8   BOUGAINVILLEA

9   FRAGRANCE BED

10   HOUSE

11   PORTE COCHERE

12   TEAK BENCH

13   FOUNTAIN

14   EUGENIA HEDGE

15   RIVER PEBBLES

16   CONCRETE BUST

17   DRIVEWAY

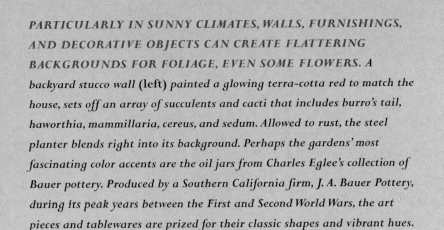

PARTICULARLY IN SUNNY CLIMATES, WALLS, FURNISHINGS, AND DECORATIVE OBJECTS CAN CREATE FLATTERING BACKGROUNDS FOR FOLIAGE, EVEN SOME FLOWERS. A backyard stucco wall (left) *painted a glowing terra-cotta red to match the house, sets off an array of succulents and cacti that includes burro's tail, haworthia, mammillaria, cereus, and sedum. Allowed to rust, the steel planter blends right into its background. Perhaps the gardens' most fascinating color accents are the oil jars from Charles Eglee's collection of Bauer pottery. Produced by a Southern California firm, J. A. Bauer Pottery, during its peak years between the First and Second World Wars, the art pieces and tablewares are prized for their classic shapes and vibrant hues.*

The signature orange-red oil jar (below), *owes its brilliance to uranium in its glaze. From it, water flows into the large pool in the back garden courtyard. Living color, in echoing orange, is supplied by the pool's population of koi (the turtle lurking in the reeds is cement). At the back, abutilon contributes dashes of yellow.*

The mosaic tabletop (below left) *was created by Nancy Kintisch, an artist friend of the owners. Its shimmering tesserae, the glass squares traditional in mosaic work since antiquity, seem to draw the California sky right down into the garden.*

DESIGNING A FOUNTAIN

It doesn't take a hydraulic engineer to get water flowing in your garden. All you need to build a fountain are a watertight receptacle, a circulating pump, and two lengths of pipe or flexible tubing—one to shoot water from the pump up through the basin, and the other one to suck it back to the pump. Though the inflow pipe, which extends above the water line and is fitted with jets, will work as a simple fountainhead, a decorative metal or masonry font provides a smoother finish for the design.

Choose the receptacle to suit the character of the setting. Anything from a dignified marble or concrete urn to a down-home galvanized tub or oak barrel (which may require a plastic liner to prevent leaking) will work. In any event, the receptacle should be wide enough to catch the fountain's splash: if the system loses too much water from spillage, this puts stress on the pump, and it will burn out over time. In a small receptacle, which tends to dry out quickly, it is prudent to use a float valve (rather like the float in a toilet). If you don't like the look of this floating object, you must be vigilant and add water as soon as the level drops. The best way to protect a fountain in winter is to turn off the pump and drain the receptacle before the first frost. Doing this will also extend the life of the pump.

A larger pump—either submersible or a surface model—produces a stronger jet. And a more expensive brass apparatus lasts much longer than its plastic counterpart. Prices range from about $40 to as much as several hundred dollars. Since no machine chugs on forever, make sure that the pump is easily accessible for repairs. An external pump housed in a sprinkler box (the concrete container that comes with an irrigation system) will be easier to service than one submerged in water or buried under rocks; it's also simpler to connect to a power source. No matter which type of pump you select, it should come equipped with a filter to keep out leaf litter, grass clippings, and other debris. Install a drain in a large fountain, for periodic cleaning.

If you want to wake to the sound of water—and what could be nicer—it's easy to add a timer that will turn on the pump at the appointed hour.

AGAINST THE WALL (right), an ancient Roman rainspout, carved in the shape of a lion's head, refills a small stone tub in Linda Allard's garden (see page 198). When water drops below a certain level, the float valve, tucked with the pump behind the wall, opens to draw more water into the system.

IN THE COURTYARD in front of the Eglee-Dalton house (far right), water gently spills over the lip of a vintage Bauer jar and into a concrete basin below. A hole drilled in the bottom of the jar admits the inflow pipe that channels water from a brass pump, housed in a gravel-lined irrigation vault situated 15 feet away. Runoff is drawn back to the pump via the outflow pipe in the pool.

A plan for the new cottage garden

IF YOU HAVE no history in your garden to begin with—say, a handy mature allée of cypress or linden trees, of the sort you might find in France or Italy—you can do what artist Gary Craig did just six years ago: create a sense of old-world structure with decidedly new-world, add-on horticultural components. His "allée," the axial link between his modest house and a distant view of far-off Mount Rainier, is a double row of dwarf Alberta spruce, set at the edges of simple beds raised above the paths between them, which give a classical grace and stature to what are, essentially, just boxes for growing vegetables.

Craig's fifteen untamed acres presented not only a design challenge (how do you impose order on a meandering, pasturelike, tree-rimmed yard?), but also an unusual scale quandary (how do you factor borrowed scenery as majestic as Mount Rainier into a cottage-scale plan?). His solution was to frame the mountain with the garden and to use human-scale geometry to stake out a claim of his own. Facing east toward the mountain from the deck that surrounds the house, a few steps descend into a 40-by-50-foot plot. There, the procession of raised beds rolls out, punctuated in the center by a simple garden pool: a cattle trough plunked into another raised bed, its corners packed with earth to hold trailing ivy and banked by daylilies, is filled with water (and goldfish), which is circulated by a pump hooked up to the house with a buried extension cord. At the far end of the raised-bed allée, a sturdy gateway arbor covered with hops, honeysuckle, and roses frames the mountain like a picture window; the central path through the arbor leads to a second arbor which, in turn, like an add-a-pearl necklace, might one day be the focus for a second cluster of raised beds—"for even more vegetables," says Craig.

The quadrangle of raised beds is an inspired design choice, both aesthetically and practically. For one thing, the two-foot-high structures mark the beds year-round, even when all that remains to anchor them are the spruce, so you always see a *garden*. Raised beds are easier on the gardener's back,

RAISED BEDS SAVE BACKS AND SOLVE SOIL PROBLEMS. No need to dig out rocks, hard-to-drain clay, or just plain poor subsoil. Beds like these, built from solid redwood planks, can be filled with soil that's custom-composed for your plants' needs. Here, dwarf Alberta spruce, bush beans and violas, carrots and rugosa roses, and herbs have happily gone to seed. Raised beds can vary in height to improve sight lines, and they're easy to weed.

the new cottage garden

A VISTA NEEDS A FRAME TO REALIZE ITS FULL POTENTIAL. Dwarf Alberta spruce lined up in two files of raised beds lead the eye to successive views, looking back toward the house (above) and from the house (previous pages) to capture the distant view of Mount Rainier. The shapely evergreens and sturdy redwood structures guarantee winter interest. Craig has fancifully chosen plants that "grow big and smell good. The structure was planned, but what went into it evolved." In one raised box, Craig grows beets, dill, and violas; in another, 'Scarlet Emperor' beans tower over more dill and poppies; a third combines a gorgeous jumble of 'White Dawn' roses with 'Red Sails' lettuce and sweet peas. On the near arbor, 'White Dawn' roses entwine with hops and two kinds of honeysuckle—Lonicera japonica 'Halliana' and L. x heckrottii. On the distant arbor, more hops curl around pink 'Blossom Time' roses.

and they're great for growing vegetables (especially root vegetables, which do best when allowed to grow straight down into deep, well-drained soil). Craig tried to keep the moles away with small-gauge chicken wire strung out under each bed at ground level, but now is forced to heavy up his defense with hardware cloth. The four quadrants lend themselves to crop rotation on a natural four-year cycle. Aesthetically, the raised beds give shape and a humble grandeur to the space as you walk among them—a garden that starts two feet up will be at least two feet higher as the crops mature. Sturdy hog fencing encloses the beds, enabling Craig to grow all kinds of vines and then pull them off when the time comes, without destroying the fence. "Hops grow 30 feet a year!" Craig exclaims. "They give you shade to sit in and hide my less-than-perfect carpentry."

In addition to inching closer to the mountain, Craig's garden spills over onto five of his fifteen acres. Roses, herbs, delphiniums, iris, and all kinds of things that smell good—"honeysuckle-y"—perennials and annuals combined, tumble out of strictly flower beds at the front of the house; more roses, a fig, and an Asian pear tree stretch out in areas outside the formal axis. Now, one of Craig's friends has built a cottage on the property, too, and an enclosed garden is planned around it. Before he bought his land, Craig had been discouraged by the ugliness of clear-cut forests in the area. Singlehandedly, he's doing his best to make up for it.

GEOMETRIC ELEMENTS DON'T REQUIRE STRICT SYMMETRY. Beds in front of the house (below) unexpectedly do not flank a path to the porch steps, so from the steps you look right into a fragrant tangle of perennials, self-seeding annuals, even a fig tree. Railings echo raised-bed structure and discourage dogs. Paths between the beds and in front of the house are lawn mower–width.

PLAN KEY

The geometry of Gary Craig's garden is both utilitarian and ornamental. Raised beds help to keep track of vegetable crop rotation, and furnish underlying structure for profuse clusters of ornamental annuals and perennials. The organizing axis of the entire plan follows a straight line from the house to the pool and on through the arbor.

1 CRAB APPLE TREES

2 ARBOR

3 DWARF EVERGREENS

4 CARROTS AND DILL

5 DWARF ALBERTA SPRUCE

6 ASIAN PEAR TREE

7 LAWN MOWER—WIDTH PATHS

8 RAISED BEDS

9 BEETS

10 TROUGH-POOL

11 DAYLILIES

12 *ROSA RUGOSA*

13 FIG TREE

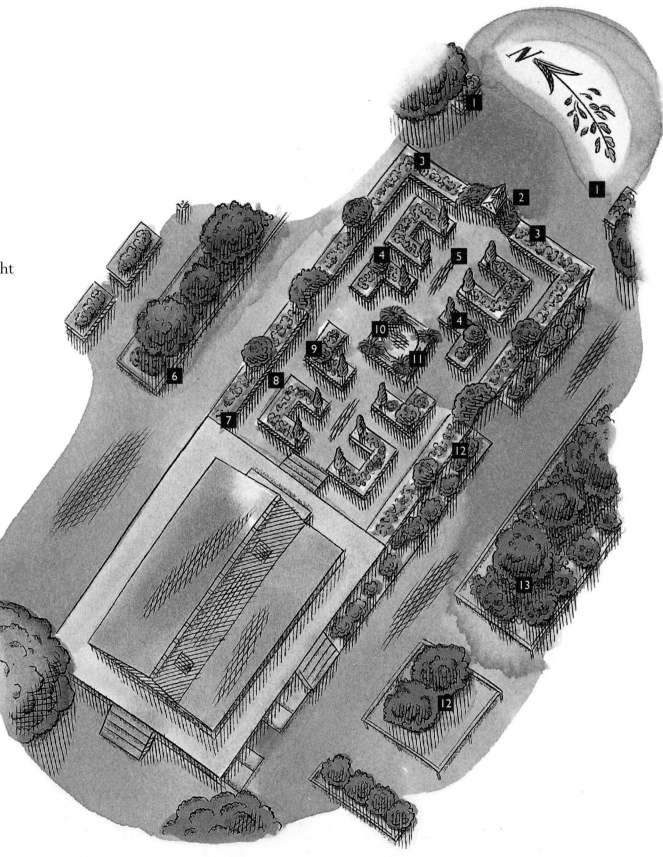

DESIGNING WITH RAISED BEDS

Beautifully crumbly, friable soil is living architecture, the best foundation for flourishing plants. Sometimes the native soil is so poor, however, that it's best to leave it behind and build gardens on top of the ground. Such is the case with intractable hardpans and caliche soils in the Southwest, bedrock in the mountains, and permanently water-logged clays in lowlands. Gary Craig's raised beds (the model for our diagram, opposite) started out as a sensible alternative to planting in stony ground. Paved yards and tarred rooftops in the city demand the same remedy. Wherever beds are used for edible crops, however, avoid chemical-infused pressure-treated wood. Because raised beds drain so fast, drip-irrigation or sprinkler systems are necessary in all but the rainiest climates. To accommodate a wheelbarrow or cart, leave four-foot paths between the boxes.

Poor soil can be improved without building boxed beds. To learn what you have to begin with, send soil samples to a testing service. In most states, soil testing is available through public cooperative extension agents for between $5 and $20. Check the Blue Pages of your phone book, under County Government. (In California, look in the Yellow Pages for a soil-testing company.) The test lab will supply mailing bags and simple instructions. The report will assess acidity, nutrients, and mineral content and let you know what you need to work into the soil for proper balance. Dolomitic limestone is a standard amendment for acidic soil. Sulfur is often prescribed for alkaline soil. Soil of any type gains essential nitrogen from additions of rotted manure as well as composted grass cuttings, leaves, straw, and fruit and vegetable scraps.

Double-digging—a time-honored, back-breaking technique—encourages deep rooting. With a spade, dig a trench 1 foot wide and 1 foot deep, putting the earth aside or in a wheelbarrow. Loosen the soil in the bottom of the trench another 12 inches with a digging fork. Then move on to the adjacent strip, digging another trench beside the first. Soil from this trench goes into the first. Dig on, transferring the top foot and loosening the lower foot. When you've finished, put the soil set aside at first into the last trench. Rake it all level, and don't tramp on those carefully fluffed beds as you work the garden.

THE STEPS TO BUILDING A RAISED BED are the same, regardless of the dimensions. Six-inch sides are tall enough if the ground below has been double-dug, though beds 2 feet high or taller require less bending over (they are also accessible to gardeners in wheelchairs). Beds 4 feet wide can be tended comfortably from either side.

1. Use lumber 1 to 2 inches thick. Cedar, redwood, and many pines are rot-resistant and will last 10 to 20 years.
2. Especially in taller beds, the soil exerts a lot of outward pressure. Fasten the sides to corner posts. Connect side boards every 4 feet with a batten, plus a brace at the top.
3. Exclude gophers, groundhogs, and other invaders by adding wire mesh to the bottom of the bed.
4. Set the frame at ground level; burying it will hasten decomposition.
5. Fill with soil high in compost and other organic matter.

A plan for classic simplicity

LIKE A STATUE FIRMLY mounted on a pedestal, Albert Hadley's house—"Italianate Victorian," as he describes it, but with a comfortable, all-American back porch—meets the ground at precise right angles. His small garden, in a palette of mostly greens, unrolls around it and ends in crisp, well-defined edges, except for one woodland path that takes you deeper, suggesting that there's space and garden to discover far beyond what you see. A study in pure symmetry, painstaking artistry, and deliberate simplicity, this garden feels as if it's been here forever, much the way the interiors Hadley designs for Parish-Hadley, his legendary design firm, bring to mind words like quality, agelessness, gentility, subtlety, classicism, and style. It's a quiet, reflective garden, on the one hand, but it would also, on the other, be a great place for a party. I'd definitely wear linen.

That the house stands within the historic district of Southport, Connecticut, makes the air of timelessness that the garden conveys seem all the more fitting. "I'm very keen on having things blend in," the designer says, with a trace of a Tennessee accent, "and here I feel obliged to." Collaborating from the beginning with an artist-sculptor friend, Mark Sciarrillo, Hadley knew that he wanted "a sense of overgrown formality." He also knew he wanted low maintenance (a garden to putter in, not one he'd have to tend every day); a garden to enhance his house, and vice versa; and results as close as possible to instant.

To both designers, formal meant flat, given the simple lines of the house and the requirements of the symmetry they were aiming for. And flat meant that the land, which sloped asymmetrically, had to be leveled. Leveling the front highlighted the house's brick foundation, so to echo it, they chose brick for the low wall bordering the square expanse of lawn that was leveled at the back. Beyond the lawn's rectangular frame, where slopes were left uneven and planted with woodland flora, a few stone steps lead you down to a clearing: a small flagstone terrace, quite simple, adorned with a scallop-edged stone birdbath.

The brick parapet, the perfect height for sitting (except that linen tends to wrinkle), is capped with bluestone, the contrasting stone that Hadley and Sciarrillo used to delineate all formal areas of the garden. They curved it to scribe a circle around the pool in the center of the back lawn, and they stretched it out into straight lines to square off the lawn. "We had to do the stonework three

266

A RESTRAINED PALETTE OF COLORS AND MATERIALS CREATES BOTH IMPACT AND SERENITY IN A SMALL SPACE. *This 50-by-50-foot back garden plays multiple variations on the color green. Foliage, in shades and textures from pale to dark, glossy to velvety, bold to subtle, is contrasted and mingled to create a complexity that intrigues but does not fatigue the eye. Flowers, mostly white, are seasonal and fleeting. Bluestone flags compose all the paving, walls are brick with bluestone coping, and garden ornaments like the birdbath and finials are harmonizing stone.*

267

times," says Hadley, "to get it right." Such symmetry requires perfectionism.

Formal, low-maintenance, and directly on axis with the living room is the garden's centerpiece—the pool and its fountain. Water rises from a stone sculpture suggesting a millstone, and ripples in concentric

A mirror, strategically placed like a false window, reflects the garden's colors, moods, and seasonal changes.

circles out to the edge of the pool, which is set in a square of ivy, its corners marked with ball finials. Ten feet in diameter (and only a few inches deep), the pool dominates the lawn, and it's meant to, adapting one of Hadley's tenets of interior design: "A large object makes a small room appear bigger."

He chose the infinitely varied greens of his garden's foliage for their "patina of age." He explains, "I have flowers, but only in tubs and pots. You can achieve wonders with greenery: glossy, matte, different shapes and textures." Another way to suggest venerability is with shape. "Misshapenness gives a pleasing sense of age, and at the nurseries I chose things that were old and overlooked. Customers don't want them if they aren't 'perfect,' but the worst-looking plants can make the best counterpoint to classical symmetry." In other words, symmetry, especially in nature, works best if it's just the

tiniest bit off. "Some things must be allowed to rumple," Hadley says. "You want a sense of order, not of perfection." So linen can be permitted to wrinkle, just a bit.

ONE BIG, HANDSOME GESTURE MAKES A SPACE SEEM LARGER. Exactly in the middle of the square back garden, this shallow pool, 10 feet in diameter and framed in bluestone flags, is set in a bed of English ivy 16 feet square, also framed in bluestone. A fountain by Mark Sciarrillo bubbles at the center of the pool; stone spheres mark the square's corners. From back porch or garden bench, this imaginative geometry anchors the symmetrical plan.

269

A BACKGROUND OF DENSE; INFORMAL PLANTING CAN ENHANCE BY CONTRAST CRISPLY DELINEATED SPACES. *Geometric gardens are by definition readable at a glance. Leaving—or making—part of a yard wild adds mystery, here intensified by the iron deer just visible at the top of the steps. Lush variegated hostas and pink rhododendrons flank this entrance to the encircling woodland, which also serves to screen out neighbors.*

PLAN KEY

First-time visitors tend to assume that the entire garden is formally contained within concentric squares around the pool. A bird's-eye view, however, reveals a subtle counterpoint of calculated informality, from the off-center lotus tree within the quadrangle to the serpentine woodland path.

I   BIRDBATH

2   IRON DEER

3   BALL FINIAL

4   ENGLISH IVY

5   BENCH

6   LOTUS TREE

7   WOODLAND PATH

8   OBELISK

9   MYRTLE

10 IRON URN

11 IRON DOG

12 LAWN

DESIGNING WITH ORNAMENTS

Useful or purely ornamental, decorative objects—pots and urns, troughs and jars, benches and seats, birdbaths and fountains, sundials and gazing balls, columns, obelisks, finials, and statues—serve as punctuation marks in a garden's design. Many of the traditional options, each suited to its place in the landscape plan, appear in Albert Hadley's garden, making it a textbook for successful use of objects. Just how many nonplant accents a garden needs (or its owner wants) is a matter of personal taste, however. If you want to use as many as Hadley does in a single acre without generating clutter, you must proceed slowly, with careful consideration of scale, color, and placement. Some householders have even successfully turned their plots, small as well as large, into open-air sculpture galleries and, in a reversal of the usual relationship, made the plants the frame for the ornaments.

Whether a garden design is formal or naturalistic, decorative objects can close a vista or draw the eye outward, mark a transition between two different spaces or emphasize the central motif, clarify a plan or spring a surprise, add charm or introduce drama. Chairs and benches are special: they can do any of the above while providing what every garden needs—places to stop and sit, look around, and dream. An ornament also makes an endearing monument, whether it's a concrete cherub that recalls marble putti in the villa where you honeymooned or a cement birdbath that marks the grave of a beloved cat.

Pieces with a linear character—wire chairs and baskets, armillary spheres, some abstract sculptures—are more effective against finely textured, single-color backgrounds. Solid shapes, whatever material they are made of, will stand up to, and often pull together, a complex mixture of colors and textures.

In Hadley's design, he has relied on classic forms and materials—cast iron, carved stone, wood, terra-cotta. However, modern designs in contemporary materials can play the same roles and are subject to the same artistic considerations. Although he has filled most of his urns and jars with plants, such containers often have equal decorative impact when they are left plant-free. Placed in the center of an open space such as a lawn or a paved terrace, one giant empty oil jar can seem to fill the surrounding space with haunting resonance.

CLASSIC SHAPES play classic roles to create a lively drama in Albert Hadley's garden.

1. A white-painted cast-iron vase planted with variegated hosta lights up a nook beside the driveway. The niche, which provides a focal point for the path from the front porch, is delineated by an arc of pavers and mown grass.
2. Overflowing with ornamental kale, one of a pair of Victorian iron urns ceremoniously flanks the front step. Also paired, but less formal: iron dogs lounge on the porch.
3. An obelisk is a time-honored eye-catcher. This one, of wood, is set directly in the line of sight of a dining-room window and thereby defines the view.
4. Real ferns brush a reproduction fern-back iron bench, which faces a twin across the lawn, reinforcing the symmetry of the plan.
5. Ornaments can migrate. The urn terminating the principal vista from the back porch, shown in this photograph, has since been replaced by the birdbath shown on page 267.

A plan for
the kitchen
garden

IT'S A TOUCH REMINISCENT of old New England, crushed oyster shells glistening in the sun on the garden path around a farm trough fed by a fountain. From this central focal point, Read and Marianne Langenbach's parterre stretches out in a neat quadrangle, its design "farm formal," as Read puts it. But the garden is on the other side of the continent from the New England of the couple's childhood memories. The Langenbachs, both transplanted easterners, bought their weekend farm on one of the San Juan Islands, northwest of Seattle, about twenty years ago, and for years they made do with a utility garden nowhere near their house. When they decided to move the garden closer, they decided, too, that it should become a room—a complex and surprising room. Pragmatism dictated the planning. Foremost, the garden had to be fenced to protect it from deer. It had to be low-maintenance, since the owners are weekend gardeners. And it had to be expansive enough—and flexible enough in design—to accommodate a mix of both ornamental and edible plants.

For all the Langenbachs' East Coast memories, though, the garden they staked out has a bold frontier spirit, offering a reassuring sense of security from the wilder areas beyond. Concentrated in a sweep of land below the house, the garden has a view of Puget Sound beyond a pasture where sheep and llamas graze. Read designed the garden first on paper, a 40-by-80-foot rectangle, divided in a geometric pattern of quadrants with a border around the perimeter, a cross-path, and the farm trough as a central focus. Aside from the oyster shells around the trough, the paths are grassy and wide enough for a lawn mower to make its way from one red-painted gate to the other. (The farm takes its name, Redgate, from those gates.) The garden gates and other structural

SEGREGATING EDIBLES FROM FLOWERS IS A WORN-OUT VEGETABLE PLOT. Vegetables, herbs, and flowers for cutting mingle decoratively and productively in each quadrant of this parterre garden centered on a pool made from a farm trough and framed in crushed oyster shells. A pump delivers water through a fountain to the pool's combination of watercress, **Iris pseudacorus,** *and* **Typha minima.**

*TO KEEP ANIMALS OUT OF THE GARDEN,
STUDY THEIR HABITS AND DESIGN
FENCES TO SUIT. Several pests demand a
combination of tactics. Rabbits enter at ground
level; so boards, chicken wire, and rocks line the
bottom of the fence to foil them. Chicken wire and
field wire layered on the 4½-foot post-and-rail
fence frustrate nibbling llamas, and a single TV
cable wire run around finial-topped posts at 7
feet deters deer. They won't try to jump, it seems,
through the 2½-foot gap between fence and wire.*

277

the kitchen garden

elements were a collaboration between the Langenbachs and a gifted carpenter who stayed in one of their barns for a while. Another rustic New England touch is the potting shed at an edge of the garden, formerly a sleeping cottage for Read and Marianne's daughters, whose antique door and shutters were salvaged in Vermont. A decidedly unrustic touch is the solar panel (found, after much searching, on nearby Orcas Island) that powers the fountain feeding the trough.

Perennials and biennials are planted against the fence and outside border, while vegetables, lavender, more perennials, annuals, and herbs fill the quadrants. Only the lavender is considered fixed; every other plant can be—and is—moved. Two espaliered apple trees anchor the garden's tractor gate, and grapevines climb the split-rail fence alongside the llama pasture. "We were never trying to maximize production," Marianne says, "but to have fun with it." Even so, the garden teems with abundant life, because Marianne believes that packing in the plants deters weeds—and also provides plenty of food not only for family and friends, but to donate to a Seattle food bank.

Although some elements seem formal, such as the lavender hedge that lines the main path, one never has the feeling of formal-by-design. This is instead a garden that makes you want to plunge in among the plants—pick things and eat them on the spot, gather them for the kitchen, make spur-of-the-moment bouquets, pick flowers to dry (as Marianne does with the larkspur), or hang around long enough to watch them change color. This is a garden meant to be used, not roped off like a museum exhibit.

Marianne, a Master Gardener, especially likes the effects of combining vegetables, herbs, and flowers in a seemingly abracadabra way. Thus sweet corn ("planted for its architectural structure and because it's appropriate in a farm garden") sometimes rises above the perennials, and gaudy bush sunflowers are mixed in with flowers that elsewhere might seem a little too restrained to work as companion plantings. Garlic with an unusual, corkscrew top grows like a natural topiary, with cosmos, lettuce, salvia, squash, and snapdragons. Globe artichokes blossom purple like the thistles they are. Tepees for pole beans and runner beans are moved every year, replenishing nitrogen in the soil. "We rotate crops in an instinctive, not a technical, way, for disease control and to balance the soil nutrients," Marianne says.

As a tribute to her New England heritage, she has planted bayberries from Cape Cod and cranberries (the latter a dismal failure). Read's 'New Dawn' rose reminds him of his father's rose garden back east—and reminds him, too, that he doesn't want a high-maintenance garden where he'd have to tend those roses constantly. He and Marianne dug a duck pond nearby, which they have planted with irises, cardinal flowers, cattails, paper birches, and willows, all meant to create a habitat that wildlife will prefer to the kitchen garden. In their hearts, though, both gardeners know that they're never out of sight of hungry eyes.

A 6-foot lean-to, dragged from elsewhere on the farm, has an antique door and shutters from Vermont, and became a potting shed after the Langenbachs' young daughters outgrew it.

PACKING BEDS TIGHTLY WITH PLANTS LEAVES NO ROOM FOR WEEDS. Such dense planting also produces a wonderfully luxuriant look, but it's a technique that works best when the soil is rich and well drained. Since this site was originally boggy, the Langenbachs installed a French drain—a ditch lined with perforated pipe and crushed stone—in the pasture just beyond the kitchen-garden fence. The soil is well manured, but some crops still have to be rotated to preserve its health.

PLAN KEY

Within the seemingly casual landscape of an American farm, utilitarian necessity provides patterns for visually satisfying design. The alignment of the kitchen garden with fences, the barnlike house (*above*), orchard, and outbuildings strikes a simple note of unforced harmony.

1 GUEST COTTAGE

2 ORCHARD

3 LLAMA BARN

4 PASTURE

5 SPLIT-RAIL FENCE

6 STREAM

7 POND

8 BENCH

9 HOUSE

10 DECK

11 WEEPING WILLOW

12 BLUEBERRIES

13 KITCHEN GARDEN

14 POTTING SHED

15 COMPOST BINS

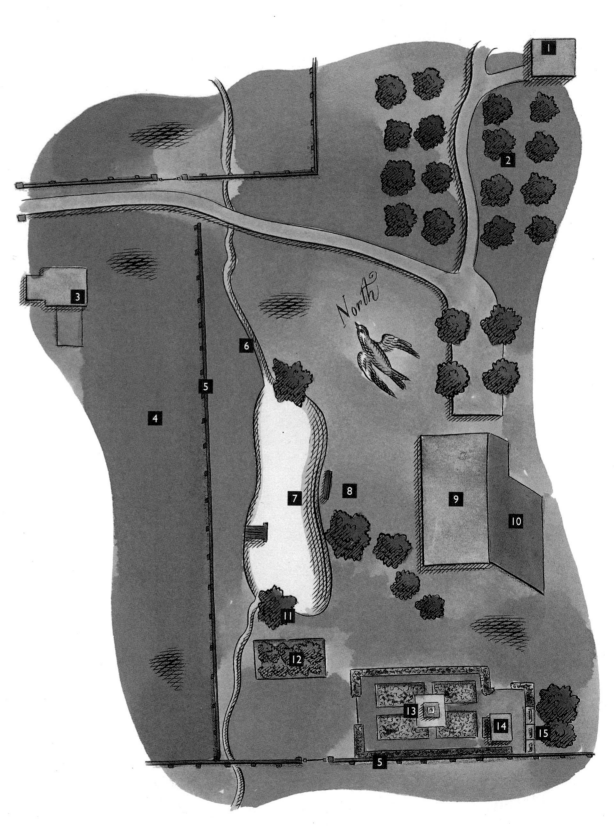

ALLOW UNRESTRAINED AND
BILLOWING PLANTS TO SOFTEN
GEOMETRIC BEDS, THEN HARVEST
WITH ABANDON. *In a precisely laid out
vegetable patch, harvesting just one head of
lettuce can spoil the pattern. In this teeming
take on the traditional jardin potager, there's
so much to look at that removing a row—or
cutting an armload of cleome, sunflowers, pink
cosmos, and larkspur—can pass unnoticed. The
only disciplined inhabitants are the grapevines
and apple trees trained against the fence.*

VEGETABLES WITH BOLD
FORMS AND DRAMATIC
FOLIAGE DESERVE TO BE
GROWN PURELY FOR
ORNAMENTAL PURPOSES.
*Shooting up like Roman candles,
globe artichokes dominate their
corner of the garden (left). The
Langenbachs don't harvest all
the buds for the table so they can
enjoy the brilliant purple
blossoms of this thistle kin. And
in the search for showstopping
foliage, you don't need to raid the
tropics.* **Right:** *Yellow crook-neck
squash does the trick and delivers
a delicious bonus as well.*

Nestled among aromatic herbs, the birdbath, like many of the garden's structures, was imaginatively improvised from a turned wooden post topped by a terra-cotta saucer.

DESIGNING THE EDIBLE GARDEN

The kitchen garden should be designed as carefully as the kitchen, with easy access and efficient work flow in mind. A permanent network of paths reduces compaction—and tilling—of the rich soil in beds. Avoid laying out paths narrower than two feet across. A four-foot width allows the passage of wheelbarrows and lets two gardeners work side by side. Brick and stone surfaces are handsome and durable, but expensive and labor-intensive. Grass paths are a less expensive alternative (sow a noninvasive bunching grass such as turf-type tall fescue), as are paths of mulch, bark chips, or gravel, which don't need mowing.

Because two feet is the maximum comfortable distance most adults can reach, beds beside fences should not exceed that depth from front to back; beds that are accessible from all sides should be no more than four feet across. The length of a bed depends on the gardener's ambition, though it's essential to put in cross-paths that let the gardener move from bed to bed easily.

Planning many separate beds encourages rotation of crops, a time-proven practice for reducing soil diseases: closely related crops, such as tomatoes and peppers or broccoli and cabbage, should never be planted in the same garden area in successive years. Mixing up vegetables, with several types planted in close proximity, is more than an aesthetic principle: It creates useful microclimates. A progression of lettuces, from early to late varieties, will thrive despite heat if they're shaded by tomatoes or trellised squash. Late-planted pole beans ramble happily through stalks of early sweet corn. Put taller plants—summer squash, artichokes, corn, dill—in mid-bed. Surround them with herbs, low-growing root crops, lettuces, and peppers. Blue or red cabbages and kales, as well as chartreuse and red lettuces, are superb for painting garden patterns with leaves. Edible nasturtium flowers add color, and decorative annuals, such as zinnias, marigolds, cosmos, and sunflowers, make the kitchen plot a cutting garden, too.

Protect and organize the kitchen garden with structures of wood and wire. Fences are a priority because they hold deer and rabbits at bay, and double as support for climbers. Inside, trellises and arches give vines the room they need to stretch; they also provide a vertical dimension that lasts through all four seasons.

THE NEW KITCHEN GARDEN: SMALL SCALE

This updated classic plan works beautifully in tight spaces. The crops are arranged for their compatibility. 1. Arugula (followed by basil); 2. red cabbage; 3. chives; 4. violas; 5. potted scented geranium; 6. cilantro (then bush beans); 7. 'Ruby Red' chard; 8. carrots; 9. nasturtiums; 10. carrots; 11. nasturtiums; 12. potted bay tree; 13. snap peas (then runner beans); 14. potted English lavender; 15. lemon basil; 16. signet marigolds; 17. 'Spicy Globe' basil; 18. oregano; 19. signet marigolds; 20. pepper; 21. tomato; 22. pepper; 23. 'Genovese' basil; 24. 'Bibb' lettuce (then bush beans); 25. potted rosemary; 26. radishes (then bush beans); 27. 'Ruby' lettuce; 28. radishes (then bush beans); 29. dill; 30. bush cucumber; 31. eggplant; 32. cherry tomato.

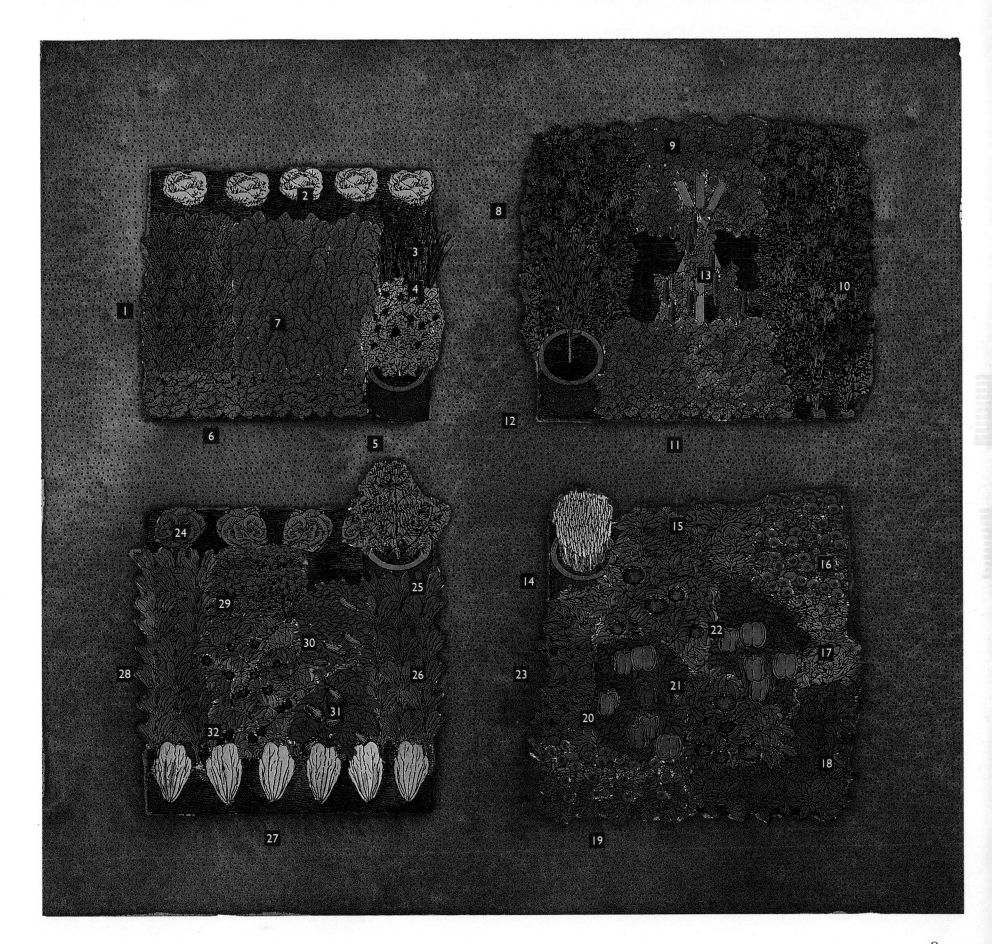

THE NEW KITCHEN GARDEN: THE WORKS

When ecology-conscious gardeners of the 1960s rejected the standard row garden, which was designed to be tilled with power equipment, they replaced it with the more intensively planted handmade raised beds of French market gardeners (see page 264 for more on raised beds). Our version, a gorgeous quilt, mingles old and new varieties of edibles: lettuces from heat-tolerant heirloom 'Red Deer Tongue' to modern 'Rosalita' and 'Bibb'; apples from venerable 'St. Johnsbury' to newcomer 'Liberty'; tomatoes from classic 'Brandywine' to contemporary disease-resistant (and tasty) 'Celebrity', 'Early Cascade', and 'Super Sweet 100'. There are boundless choices for delectable color: chartreuse 'Minaret' broccoli, 'Violet Queen' cauliflower, 'Purple Ruffles' basil, 'Golden' beets, and rosy 'Rosa Bianco' eggplant.

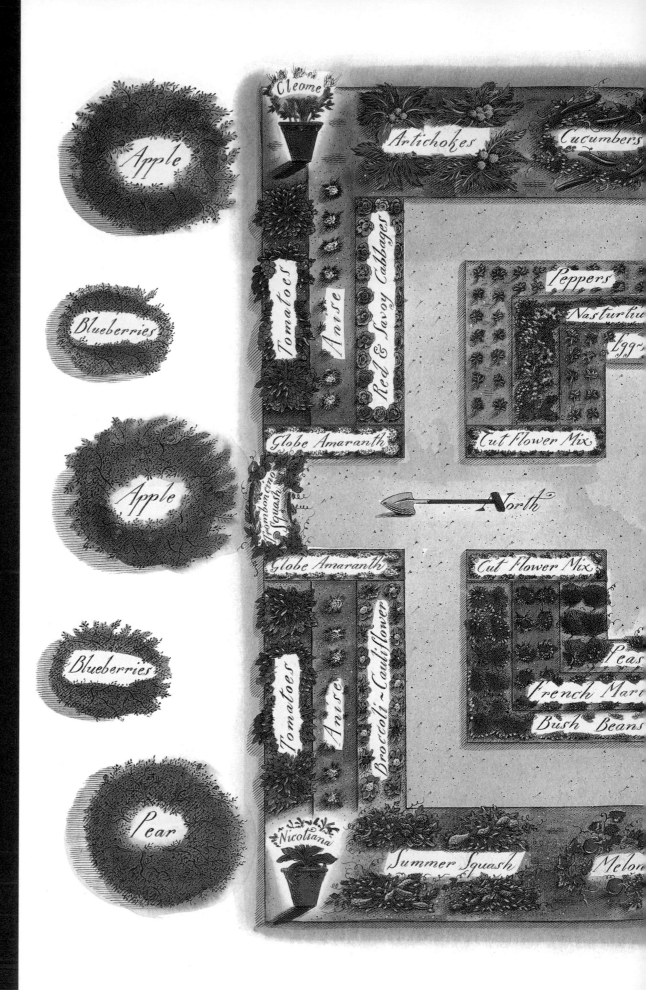

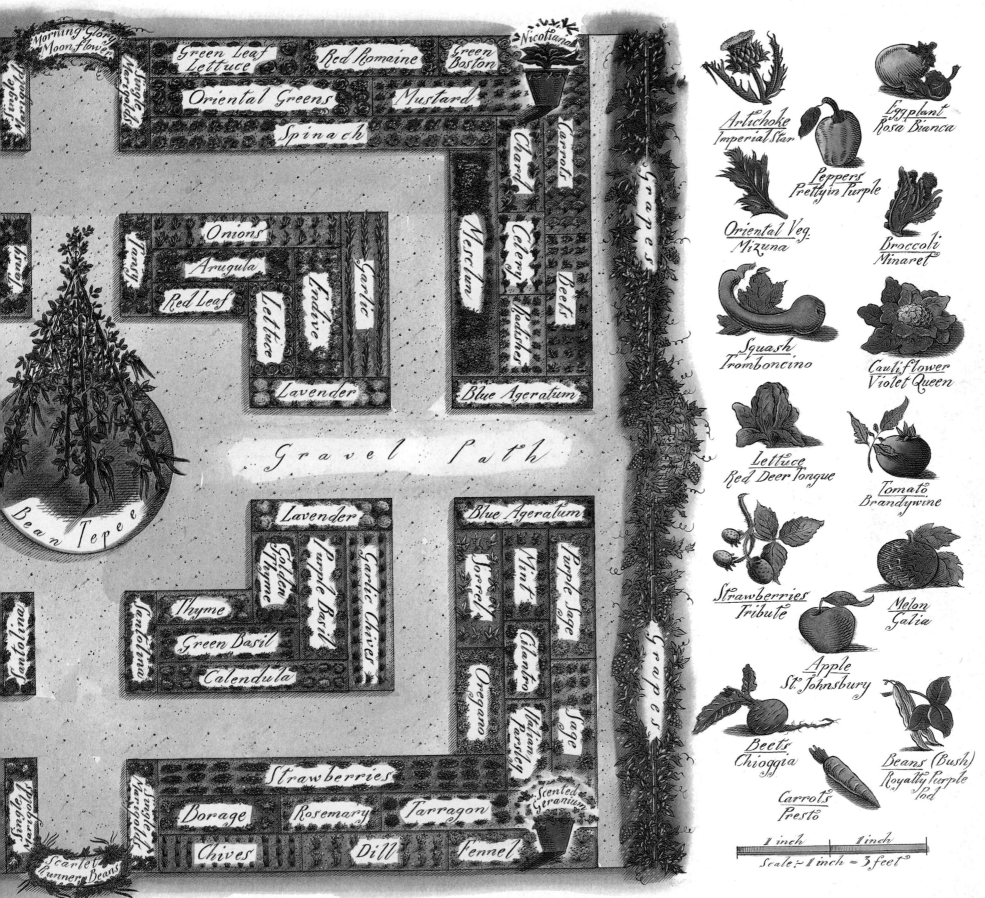

A plan for American formality

THE NATIVES-VERSUS-EXOTICS debate, by far the hottest horticultural issue of the '90s, has left many an American gardener feeling tired, torn, and guilty. We want to do the environmentally correct thing. We've tried to stop worshipping unattainable British ideals. But sometimes an unruly meadow just won't do when you desire a neat stretch of clipped lawn; native species often seem too informal for elegant effects; and it's tough to discriminate against beauty on the basis of national origin. If you think you have to make a decision and come down hard on one side or the other, think again. More than seventy years before we began the current round of ecological bickering, a renowned American landscape architect, Lockwood de Forest, had already discovered a patch of middle ground in California—where he created regionally sensitive gardens planted with native species *and* exotics suited to the southwestern climate. Today, Carol and David Geyer are keeping his legacy intact at the Santa Barbara house and garden that de Forest and his wife, Elizabeth (who shared his vision and became a landscape architect, too), created for their own family in 1926.

De Forest's genius lay in the art of compromise. He took dusty California colors and interpreted them with introduced species—from South Africa, the Mediterranean, China, Japan, Australia, any place with similar growing conditions—in such a way that these outsiders felt, and looked, at home in their new landscapes. He stretched European structure to fit the Wild West. Instead of a yew hedge, de Forest would clip eugenia to make a similar architectural statement. If he wanted a formal lawn, he planted drought-tolerant African grass and refused to let anyone water it. (Though the lawn might not stay green year-round, he learned to appreciate its tan hues during dry seasons.) De Forest also felt that California was too big for gardens with the traditional precise beginnings and ends. In his opinion, gardens made to embrace distant views belong more naturally to a wide-open landscape than do gardens ending with an arbitrary property line. So his designs weren't drawn with a ruler, but painted with brush strokes; the strokes are strong and confident, though on occasion they blur a bit, just like nature.

For his own home, de Forest bought a mere acre of land in Mission Canyon and designed a house (which is, not surprisingly, a West Coast take on Roman architecture) and a garden with an axial view toward La Cumbre Peak—a view that seems to go on forever. Thus, from many vantage points, the eye climbs the landscape as if it were a staircase to hedges and treetops (first inside and then outside the garden), to the mountain, and back to the tranquility of de Forest's private space. Though

IMAGINATIVELY PLACED,
THE TRADITIONAL CLIPPED
TREES AND SHRUBS OF
FORMAL GARDENING CAN
CREATE STRUCTURE WITHOUT
RIGIDITY. *Precisely sheared globes
of myrtle and billowing perennials
turn a narrow garden into a
rhythmic progression of surprises.
Plantings on either side of the path
are symmetrically balanced but not
identical: scented geraniums face
Santa Barbara daisies, the
counterpart to a clipped hedge of
variegated pittosporum.*

289

Ornamental grapes overhang the front entrance to the house, where jasmine flowers beside the stone stairs.

PLAN KEY

An exquisite melding of straight lines and curves, symmetry and asymmetry, plots an almost seamless progression from the formality of the house and its immediate surroundings to the free-flowing contours of rougher terrain outside the property. The design adapts refined European style to American expansiveness.

1 ROSEMARY

2 KOI POND

3 LAVENDER GARDEN

4 COASTAL LIVE OAK

5 KIKUYU LAWN

6 OLIVE TREE

7 FOUNTAIN

8 ROSE GARDEN

9 GRAPE ARBOR

10 REFLECTING POOL

11 CHILDREN'S PLAYGROUND

12 ENTRANCE COURT

13 SERVICE COURT

14 ART STUDIO

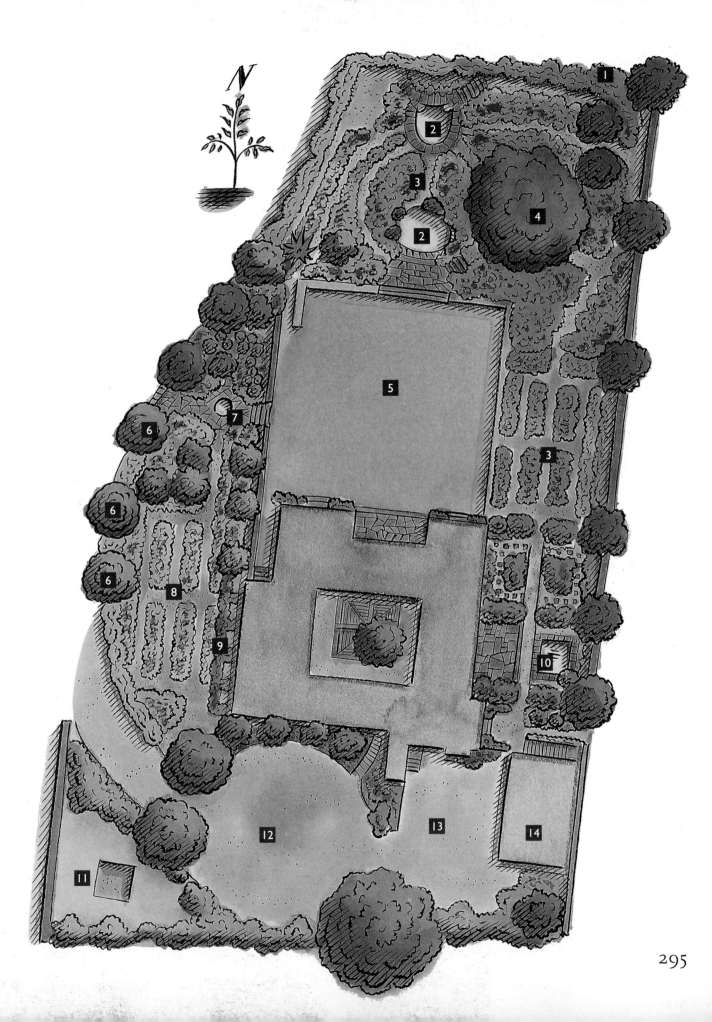

DESIGNING FOR YOUR REGION

We often form our images of what a garden should be early in life. If we grew up with acres of green lawn and tall trees or loved our grandmother's rose- and delphinium-stuffed flower beds, we instinctively try to give ourselves the same surroundings even when we move to a different part of the country with a different climate. Moving is something we Americans do a lot. And we are beginning to realize that when we're in an unfamiliar location, we need to do some research to plan our gardens well. We need to know about the availability of water, the acidity or alkalinity of the soil, the extremes of heat and cold, and the native flora in our new neighborhoods, then make choices accordingly.

The late J. C. Raulston, whose life's work at North Carolina State University was introducing people to new plants for landscaping, always maintained that gardeners should garden where they live, not someplace else. Too often we bring a plant into our gardens just because we like it, even though it will have to struggle to look half bad. Sure, you can raise tropicals in the Adirondacks if you're willing to haul them inside each winter, or have a Kentucky bluegrass lawn in the Badlands if you're willing to pay the water bill, but why bother when more suitable plants thrive with less effort and look as if they actually belong there?

Regional natives have advantages over some exotic imports. Natives are comfortable with the local climate, bugs, and soil conditions. If they grow wild near you without help, think how well they'll do with a little attention.

You may find that confining yourself strictly to natives is too limiting. Perhaps you want colors or shapes that natives don't supply or bloom at a time when they are having a rest period. In that case, look for *appropriate* plants that are indigenous to a region similar to yours. Plants that grow in similar climates tend to look better together because they evolved under the same conditions. We, as gardeners, have also come to see various types of Mediterranean vegetation, for example, or inhabitants of the tropics, as suitable companions.

Many of us are lucky enough to be able to look through our property and out onto a natural vista. If the plant matter we have chosen integrates well with the surroundings, our garden feels larger and more at home. And so do we.

A MEETING OF DESERT DWELLERS from South Africa and North America creates glowing color in a Southern California hillside garden (*right*) designed by Tim Galardi of Riviera Gardens. At ground level, *Echeveria* 'Afterglow' and golden barrel cactus add yellow tints to African yellow-green *Crassula* 'Campfire' and gray senecio. Spiky accents include African aloes; their American cousins, agaves; and native ocotillo.

LUXURIANT TROPICAL DENIZENS mingle with south Florida natives (*far right*) in Brian Morris's beautifully structured jungle in Miami. Exotic bromeliads and staghorn ferns join indigenous Spanish moss on native trees, while south Asian fishtail palms screen the perimeter.

index

U.S. Department of Agriculture Plant Hardiness Zone Map

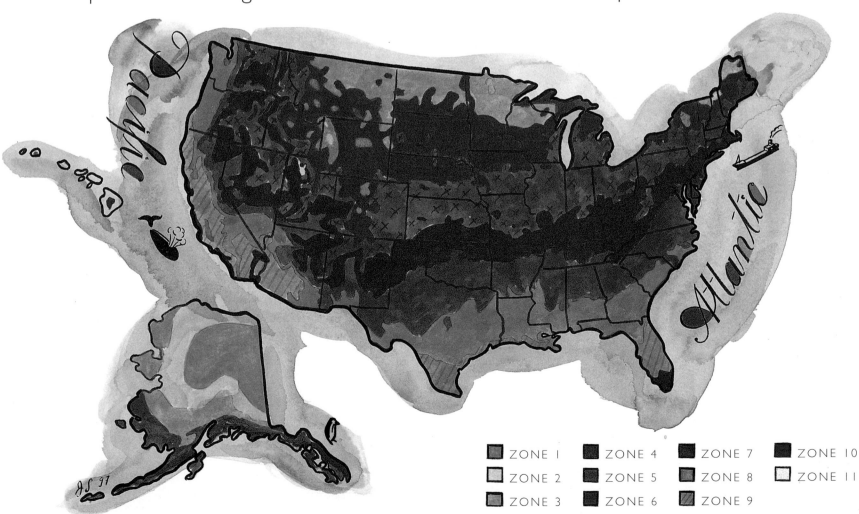

ZONE 1 ZONE 4 ZONE 7 ZONE 10
ZONE 2 ZONE 5 ZONE 8 ZONE 11
ZONE 3 ZONE 6 ZONE 9

credits

KEY: T = top, B = bottom, L = left,
C = center, R = right